THIS IS OUR YOUTH

BY **KENNETH LONERGAN**

★

★

DRAMATISTS
PLAY SERVICE
INC.

THIS IS OUR YOUTH
Copyright © 1999, Kenneth Lonergan

All Rights Reserved

SPECIAL NOTE

THIS IS OUR YOUTH was produced by The New Group (Scott Elliot, Artistic Director; Claudia Catania, Executive Producer) at The INTAR Theatre in New York City in October 1996. It was directed by Mark Brokaw. The cast was as follows:

DENNIS ZIEGLER .... Josh Hamilton
WARREN STRAUB .... Mark Ruffalo
JESSICA GOLDMAN .... Missy Yager

THIS IS OUR YOUTH was produced by Second Stage Theatre (Carole Rothman, Artistic Director; Carol Fishman, Managing Director; Alexander Fraser, Executive Director), by special arrangement with Barry and Fran Weissler and The New Group (Scott Elliot, Artistic Director; Claudia Catania, Executive Producer), in New York City in November 1998. The production subsequently transferred to The Douglas Fairbanks Theatre under the auspices of Barry and Fran Weissler and Eric Krebs. It was directed by Mark Brokaw; the set design was by Allen Moyer; the costume design was by Michael Krass; the lighting design was by Mark McCullough; the sound design was by Robert Murphy; the fight director was Rick Sordelet; and the production stage manager was William H. Lang. The cast was as follows:

DENNIS ZIEGLER .... Mark Rosenthal
WARREN STRAUB .... Mark Ruffalo
JESSICA GOLDMAN .... Missy Yager

CHARACTERS

DENNIS ZIEGLER — 21 years old

WARREN STRAUB — 19 years old

JESSICA GOLDMAN — 19 years old

TIME

The Time is late March 1982.

PLACE

The Play takes place in Dennis' one-room apartment
on the Upper West Side of Manhattan.

A NOTE ON SIMULTANEOUS DIALOGUE:

Double dialogue laid out in side-by-side columns is meant to be
spoken simultaneously. I.e., the actor saying the dialogue in the
right-hand column is *not* to wait for the actor saying the dialogue
in the left-hand column to finish, but to start speaking at the exact
same time.

While in some cases absolute exactness is neither possible nor
necessary, in general the more precisely the actors try to stick to
this rule, the better the simultaneous dialogue will work.

THIS IS OUR YOUTH

ACT ONE

A cold Saturday night in March 1982, after midnight. A small impersonal pillbox studio apartment on the 2nd or 3rd floor of a somewhat rundown postwar building on the Upper West Side of Manhattan between Broadway and West End, lived in by Dennis Ziegler. There is a TV and stereo, a lot of records, some arbitrary furniture, a little-used kitchenette and a mattress on the floor in the corner. Scattered around the room are piles of the New York Post, *sports magazines, and a lot of underground comic books. There is sports equipment in the apartment, if not actually in view. The room looks lived-in, but aside from a wall of photographs from Dennis' life, no effort whatsoever has been made to decorate it. It looks like it could be packed up and cleared out in half an hour. Dennis is watching TV. He is a grungy, handsome, very athletic formerly long-haired kid, just twenty-one years old, wearing baggy chino-type pants and an ancient polo shirt. He is a very quick, dynamic, fanatical and bullying kind of person; amazingly good-natured and magnetic, but insanely competitive and almost always successfully so; a dark cult god of high school only recently encountering, without necessarily recognizing, the first evidence that the dazzling aggressive hipster techniques with which he has always dominated his peers might not stand him in good stead for much longer. The buzzer buzzes. Dennis is too cool to answer it right away. It buzzes again. He gets up and goes to the intercom.*

DENNIS. Yeah?

WARREN. *(Over the intercom.)* Yo, Dennis. It's me, Warren.

DENNIS. What do you want?

WARREN. *(Over the intercom.)* Yo, lemme up.

> *Dennis hits the buzzer. Sits down and watches TV. There is a knock at the door. Again, he doesn't answer it right away. Another knock.*

(From off.) Yo, Denny.

> *Dennis gets up and unlocks the door without opening it, then plops down again to watch TV. Warren Straub comes in the front door. He is a skinny nineteen-year-old; a strange barking dog of a kid with large tracts of thoughtfulness in his personality that are not doing him much good at the moment, probably because they so infrequently influence his actions. He has spent most of his adolescence in hot water of one kind or another, but is just beginning to find beneath his natural eccentricity a dogged self-possession his friends may not all share, and despite his enormous self destructiveness, he is above all things a trier. His language and wardrobe are heavily influenced by Dennis—but only up to a point, and he would be a good-looking kid if he eased up on his personal style a little. He comes into the apartment lugging a very big suitcase and an overloaded heavy-duty hiking backpack.*

Hey.

DENNIS. What's with the suitcase?

WARREN. Nothing… What are you doing?

DENNIS. Nothing.

> *Warren closes the door and puts down his stuff. Sits down next to Dennis on the mattress and looks at the TV.*

WARREN. What are you watching?

DENNIS. Lock the door.

> *Warren gets up and locks the door. He sits down as before.*

WARREN. What are you watching?

> *Dennis flashes off the TV with the remote control.*

DENNIS. Nothing. What do you want?

WARREN. Nothing.

DENNIS. I don't have any pot.

WARREN. I don't want any. I got some.

DENNIS. Let me see it.

> *Warren produces a ziplock plastic bag carefully wrapped around a small amount of dark green marijuana. Dennis opens it and smells it.*

This is good. Where'd you get it?

WARREN. From Christian.

DENNIS. Can we smoke it?

WARREN. I'm saving it.

DENNIS. For what?

> *Dennis takes the pot out of the bag and reaches for a record album. He starts to crumble the pot onto the album cover.*

WARREN. Just half.

DENNIS. Shut up.

WARREN. Just *half*, man.

> *Dennis looks at him and crumbles the rest of the pot onto the album.*

DENNIS. You got papers?

WARREN. You're a fuckin' asshole.

> *He gets up. Dennis laughs.*

DENNIS. There's some papers on the table. Gimme one.

> *Warren does not comply.*

(*Sharply.*) Hey! Give me a *rolling* paper. Do you know how much money you owe me?

> *Warren takes out a small wad of bills, peels off a few and drops them on the bed.*

Where'd you get this?

WARREN. What do you care?

DENNIS. Well if you're so rich then you can get more pot from Christian tomorrow, so give me the fucking rolling papers before I beat the shit out of you.

> *Warren goes to the table and throws a packet of Club or*

Zig-Zag rice papers to Dennis.

What happened, Jasonius kicked you out?

WARREN. No, man, I left.

DENNIS. You can't stay here.

WARREN. I don't want to stay here.

DENNIS. Why'd he kick you out? What'd you do?

WARREN. Nothing. I got stoned and he comes home and he's like, "This apartment smells like pot *all the time*." And I'm like, "Yeah, 'cause I'm always *smoking* it." So then he's like, "I want that smell out of this house." And then he's like, "No, actually, I want *you* out of this house." Then he throws a few bills on the floor and is like, "There's some cash, now pack up your shit and get out before I beat your fuckin' head in." And I was like, "Whatever." So he went on a date with his whore, and I packed up my stuff and left.

DENNIS. Where are you going to stay?

WARREN. I don't know. Maybe I'll stay with Christian. I don't know. Maybe I'll stay in a hotel. Who the hell knows?

DENNIS. How are you going to stay in a hotel?

WARREN. I got money.

DENNIS. How much did he give you?

WARREN. He gave me some money.

DENNIS. Why? Like to thank you for leaving?

WARREN. I guess.

DENNIS. How much is this?

> *Putting the beautifully rolled joint in his mouth, Dennis counts the money Warren threw on the bed.*

WARREN. Two hundred.

> *Dennis finishes counting. From under the mattress he pulls a beat-up school composition notebook and flips through it till he finds Warren's name.*

DENNIS. "Warren:" *(Writing in the book.)* "Cleared. With Stolen Funds."

WARREN. They're not stolen, man, he gave it to me.

Dennis closes the book, finds a match and lights up.

DENNIS. *(Holding in the smoke.)* Where did Christian get this from?

WARREN. I don't know.

Dennis slaps Warren in the face, playfully but hard.

DENNIS. Don't fuckin' lie to me—where'd he get it?

Warren tries to hit Dennis back but Dennis is much bigger and stronger and stops him.

WARREN. Don't fuckin' hit me—

DENNIS. Where did he get it from?

WARREN. Why don't you ask him?

DENNIS. Did he get it from Philip?

WARREN. No, he said he got it from some fuckin' Rastafarian.

DENNIS. That guy Wally?

WARREN. I don't know.

DENNIS. That guy Kresko?

WARREN. I don't know. I don't keep track of where you guys perform your criminal activities. Who cares? Gimme that.

Dennis doesn't move. He keeps smoking. Warren reaches for the joint. Dennis allows him to take it.

DENNIS. How much money did you steal?

WARREN. A lot.

DENNIS. Let me see.

Warren opens his backpack and takes out a felt shoe bag stuffed to bursting with cash. He loosens the ties and shows it to Dennis.

That's a lot.

WARREN. It's fifteen thousand dollars.

DENNIS. Are you fucking *crazy*?

Pause.

Give me half.

WARREN. No.

DENNIS. Give me *five*.

WARREN. I'm not giving you anything.

DENNIS. No. Give me five, we'll go to *France*, and we'll mail the rest back to your dad with a note. "Took five. Went to *France*."

WARREN. I'm keeping it.

DENNIS. Are you kidding? He'll send large *men* after you with *guns*.

WARREN. He doesn't even know I have it.

DENNIS. What do you mean?

WARREN. I mean he—   DENNIS. Where did you *get* it from?
It was in his room.

DENNIS. It was in his *room*?

WARREN. Yeah.

DENNIS. Your father keeps fifteen thousand dollars cash in his *room*? For what? *Tips?*

WARREN. I don't know. I guess he's got some kind of illicit lingerie deal in the works or something, I don't know.

DENNIS. Your father is so heavy, man…

WARREN. Yeah, so after he threw me out and went to *supper*, I was just roaming the house looking for liftable objects, if that was gonna be his attitude. So I go in his bedroom and there's this sinister looking *brief*case just *sitting* on his *bed*. So I jimmied open the lock and there's like rows and rows of cash just starin' at me. Like totally full of money.

DENNIS. *Jason*.

WARREN. Yeah! So I'm like, "*Dad…!*" And then I'm like, "Should I take this? This is some serious money." And then I'm like, "Fuck yeah. Make him *pay*." So I take out the cash, and I fill the briefcase with all these old *National Geographic*s and lock it up again. So it'll probably sit there for the weekend, and then when he goes to deposit it, or bribe whoever he was planning on bribing, he'll open it up and hopefully he'll think like one of his *cohorts* ripped him off. Or like, his *slut* did it.

DENNIS. No he *won't*.

WARREN. Why not?

DENNIS. Of *course* he won't.

WARREN. Why not?

DENNIS. Because he's not a *moron*.

WARREN. Yes he is.

DENNIS. You really think after he throws you out of the house he's gonna open his briefcase and find twenty copies of his own *National Geographics* where his *money* should be, and he's not gonna know you did it? You're a fuckin' moron. Now get that shit outta here.

WARREN. I'm telling you—

DENNIS. Take it over to Christian's house and let your father's bodyguards break *his* fuckin' legs.

WARREN. He doesn't *have* any bodyguards.

DENNIS. That guy who drives his car is not a bodyguard?

WARREN. No, he's a *driver*.

DENNIS. That guy like shows me his *gun*, like every time I *see* him.

WARREN. Yeah, because he's *insane*. But my father is not a *criminal*. He's just in *business* with criminals.

DENNIS. I don't give a shit *what* he is. I can't believe you cart that kind of money across town and like bring it to my *doorstep*. No—No—I mean you are so stupid, man, you are so incredibly stupid. He kicks you out so you steal fifteen thousand *dollars* from him?

WARREN. I was pissed.

DENNIS. OK: Get it out of here. Take it to Christian's house.

WARREN. He's not home.

DENNIS. Take it to Yoffie's house; go to Leonard's house. I don't care.

WARREN. Nobody's home. Everyone's parents are home. I'm not allowed in their houses. Come on. I don't want to be wandering around the streets with all that money. Come on.

DENNIS. This is so typical of you, man, I mean this is like…

WARREN. Yeah yeah yeah.

DENNIS. This is like the prototype moronic move we've all come to expect from your corner. You drive the guy *crazy* because you're such a sniveling little obnoxious punk, you *grate* on the guy until he finally throws you out—arguably the most dangerous lingerie manufacturer in the *world*—And then you steal his *money* and bring it to my *house*, and expect me to like, *hide* you or something?

Warren starts to speak.

No—No—That's why nobody likes you, man, because you're always provoking people. OK, now everybody's provoked, only *you're* the one they all fuckin' hate! Listen to me. I'm trying to tell you something. This is good for you.

WARREN. Oh, yeah.

DENNIS. No it is. It's good for you. Listen. You're a fuckin' *idiot.* You never have any money. Nobody can stand to have you around. And you can't get laid. I mean, man, you cannot get laid. You *never* get laid. Like the last girlfriend you had was in like ninth grade and it lasted for two weeks, and that bitch probably still hasn't recovered.

WARREN. She hasn't. I freaked her out.

DENNIS. What kind of *life* do you lead? You live with your father— a psycho. He beats the shit out of you on like this regular *basis*, you habitually owe me hundreds of dollars, you never pay me—until now, but we won't even discuss that—Nobody can stand to have you around because you're such an annoying loudmouthed little creep, and now you're like some kind of fugitive from *justice*? What is gonna happen to you, man?

WARREN. What's gonna happen to anybody? Who cares?

Dennis shrugs, sits. Relights the joint, which has gone out.

Like you're so independent?

DENNIS. Yeah, because my parents *pay* for this apartment. They don't throw me *out* of it. Because they're so grateful I don't wanna live with them. Because I don't *goad* them into *making* me dependent. I'm just like, "*Don't* send me to college. Just spring for my rent, I'll be a *bike* messenger till I decide what I wanna do, and we'll never have to deal with each other." And they're like, "*Fine.*"

Pause.

WARREN. Why do you say that shit?

DENNIS. Because it's true.

WARREN. Why do you—   DENNIS. Because you deserve it.

Pause. Warren is close to tears.

DENNIS. Are you *crying* now?

WARREN. No.

Pause.

I don't know what to do. *I* don't know where to go.

DENNIS. Well—for one thing you should give me five thousand dollars and then you should return that money.

WARREN. I'm not giving you five thousand dollars.

DENNIS. I'm telling you. *France.*

WARREN. You want some money?

DENNIS. No, I don't want any money.

Warren opens the bag and holds out two bricks of cash.

WARREN. Take some money. Go to fuckin' France.

DENNIS. I don't wanna go to France. Like I want your father *stalking* me for the rest of my life? Now put that shit back in the bag and take it back to where you found it. It *scares* me.

Warren puts the money back and closes the ties.

WARREN. I can't return it because he's home by now. He's *asleep.* The shit is in his bedroom and he's gonna be home all day tomorrow because he's having some associates over for *brunch.*

DENNIS. Brunch.

Pause.

That's a wild concept: It's not breakfast and it's not lunch. It's *brunch.* *(Rolls the word around in his mouth.)* "Brunch." "Let's serve *brunch...*" It's something you serve.

Long pause.

This is strong pot.

WARREN. I know.

DENNIS. All right: You know what you should tell your father?

WARREN. It doesn't matter what I do. He's gonna kill me anyway, so what's the difference?

DENNIS. No. Let's figure this out. It's gonna be OK. I'm a total mathematical genius. Now how much of this cash did you spend?

13

WARREN. Not much. I paid you back… I took a cab… I ate sushi… Two hundred and fifty bucks. But he gave me fifty.

DENNIS. OK. So don't spend any more, hang out till Monday, and then return it on Monday when he goes to work. If the briefcase is already gone, then just like, leave the cash in his bedroom with a note of explanation—and like, leave town.

WARREN. I don't know.

DENNIS. That's a sound plan. And if he still hasn't even opened the briefcase you're like home free. Except for two hundred bucks.

WARREN. Can I get the two hundred back from you?

DENNIS. No, man, that's like, *paid*. I can't release that cash.

WARREN. Where am I gonna stay?

DENNIS. Stay with Christian.

WARREN. Why can't I stay here?

DENNIS. 'Cause I don't want you.

WARREN. It's just two days.

DENNIS. I don't care.

WARREN. Come on. Nothin's gonna happen. He's not gonna know I came here. He definitely won't open the briefcase till Monday and I'll be gone by then.

DENNIS. You are so stupid, man. I mean this definitely crowns your career as an idiot.

WARREN. Just let me stay here for Christ's sakes! I do shit for you all the time—

DENNIS. Like what?

WARREN. Like when your girlfriend kicked you out, you stayed at my house for two *weeks*—

DENNIS. That was your *father's* house.

WARREN. So *what*?

DENNIS. This is *my* house.

WARREN. And I got in a lotta trouble for that, too. I hang out with you whenever you want, I play sports with you all the time, I buy pot from you, I take all your fuckin' abuse and I'm a good fuckin' friend. So why can't you help me out when I'm in trouble and not be such a fuckin' asshole?

DENNIS. 'Cause you're *always* in trouble. You have like no sense of *differentiation*.

WARREN. It's just two days!

DENNIS. All right, all right, shut up.

WARREN. Thanks.

DENNIS. But if your father shows up here I'm givin' you up immediately.

WARREN. I'm sure you will. But he's not gonna.

    Silence.

So what's up? What do you wanna do?

DENNIS. No, I don't wanna *do any*thing. Don't *needle* me, Warren. If you wanna stay here you can stay here, but you gotta shut up.

    Dennis turns on the TV and watches it wholeheartedly.

WARREN. Hey, where's that chick Jessica?

    Pause.

Denny. Have you seen that chick Jessica recently?

DENNIS. No. What about her?

WARREN. I'm into her.

DENNIS. She's out of your league, man.

WARREN. I think she likes me.

DENNIS. No she doesn't.

WARREN. I think she does.

DENNIS. Shut up.

WARREN. She's really cute, man.

DENNIS. She is cute. That's why it'll never happen.

    Warren wanders over to the fridge.

There's nothing in there.

    Warren opens the fridge and looks in.

Get outta there, Warren! I just told you there's nothing in there.

WARREN. How come you never have any food in here?

Dennis doesn't answer. He watches TV.

Let's go play football.

Dennis doesn't answer.

Where's your girlfriend?

DENNIS. We had a fight.

WARREN. Why?

DENNIS. Because she's a cunt.

WARREN. Tell her to come over and bring that girl Jessica.

DENNIS. Tell her yourself.

WARREN. *(Going to the phone.)* Where's she at?

DENNIS. You can't call her. We had a fight.

Warren picks up Dennis' football and makes phantom passes.

WARREN. Let's go outside and play.

DENNIS. Forget it.

WARREN. Let's call your girlfriend and tell her to call that girl Jessica, and we'll take a few thousand bucks out of the shoe bag and rent a really nice hotel suite and get a lot of champagne and shit and have a wild party. What do you think?

Warren throws Dennis the football. Dennis throws it back. Dennis knows how to throw a football.

DENNIS. You can't spend that money.

WARREN. I'll spend some of it. Big deal.

They toss the football back and forth.

Come on, I'll get laid. It'll be good.

DENNIS. Let's just get a couple of prostitutes.

WARREN. OK.

DENNIS. You want to? We can call this Japanese place Philip goes to and they'll send over like two incredibly beautiful and obedient Oriental hostesses to entertain and delight us.

WARREN. Let's do it.

DENNIS. How much will you spend?

WARREN. I don't know. How much is it?

DENNIS. Like two hundred apiece.

WARREN. I'd be into that.

DENNIS. What'll you tell your dad?

WARREN. Fuck my dad. I took his *money*!

DENNIS. You robbed him!

> *Warren throws a hard pass that goes wide and smashes into some breakables.*

WARREN. Whoa. Sorry.

DENNIS. What is your *problem*!?

WARREN. I lost control of the ball.

> *Dennis gets the ball out of the smashed shelfware.*

Yo. Denny. Toss it back.

DENNIS. You broke my girlfriend's sculpture.

WARREN. Whoa… Really? I'm sorry.

DENNIS. What is your *problem*?

WARREN. I don't know. I really broke it?

DENNIS. Yeah, you really *broke* it.

> *Warren comes over and examines the broken clay sculpture.*

WARREN. What was it?

DENNIS. It was two girls, makin' out.

WARREN. Intense.

DENNIS. Now it's like, half of two girls.

WARREN. I'm really sorry, man, it was an accident.

DENNIS. It's a piece of shit anyway.

WARREN. Yo, lemme see it. Maybe I can glue it back together.

DENNIS. Get away from it.

WARREN. Lemme see.

> *Warren tries to get a hand on the broken sculpture. Dennis roughly blocks him out with his body and elbows.*

DENNIS. Go sit in the *corner*, Warren, you're a fuckin' *menace*. Look what you *did*.

WARREN. Let me repair it.

Dennis can't do anything with it. He lets Warren look at it.

No problem. You just get some Krazy Glue and glue it together. Do you have any?

DENNIS. No I don't have any *Krazy* Glue.

WARREN. I can fix this.

Dennis wanders away from the shelves.

DENNIS. I'm *wasted.*

WARREN. Look. See?

He has propped the two halves of the broken sculpture together so it looks whole.

Just glue it like that and it'll be fine. You probably don't even need a clamp.

Warren picks up the football and makes phantom passes at Dennis.

Yo, heads up. Yo, Denny—go out.

DENNIS. Would you put that *down*?

WARREN. Go long!

DENNIS. The fuck am I gonna go *long*?

WARREN. Yo, go out!

Warren throws the football hard, a little out of Dennis' reach and it smashes into a bunch of other stuff.

DENNIS. What is *with* you, Warren?

WARREN. Come on, you had it!

Dennis grabs the football, rears back and wings a viciously hard pass at Warren's head. Warren ducks and the football smashes into the sculpture again, totally demolishing it.

DENNIS. *Catch* it, you *moron*! Don't *duck*! This is my *house*!

WARREN. You tried to kill me, man!

DENNIS. What is the matter with you?

WARREN. I didn't do anything!

Dennis stalks Warren, grabs him in a headlock and flings him down on the floor. They are both half-laughing.

DENNIS. Get outta my *house*!

WARREN. Come on, man, I didn't do anything!

Dennis rains open-handed blows down on Warren's head and body. Warren covers up. Dennis drops onto his gut, knee first. Warren groans in pain. Dennis gets up and looks at the wreckage.

DENNIS. Look what you *did*.

WARREN. Oh my stomach.

DENNIS. Oh, forget *this*…

He starts tossing the pieces of the sculpture, basketball-style, into the waste paper basket across the room. He's a good shot. Most of them go in.

She's gonna freak out.

The last piece goes into the wastepaper basket. Dennis walks over to it and boots it into the wall. He goes to Warren, who is covering his head.

You all right?

Warren uncovers his head. Dennis slaps him in the face.

WARREN. Cut it out.

DENNIS. That's for breaking her shit.

WARREN. You murdered my stomach.

Long silence.

I'm restless.

Dennis gives him a look.

So, you don't wanna call any Japanese hostesses?

DENNIS. You couldn't handle it. You'd go limp and be depressed about it for like a year and a half.

WARREN. Let's call 'em!

DENNIS. Shut up. It's two hundred dollars apiece. You wanna spend that cash?

WARREN. No, man, I can't.

DENNIS. What are you gonna do about the two hundred bucks?

WARREN. I don't know. I'll sell something.

DENNIS. What, from like your little faggot memorabilia collection?

19

WARREN. Yeah.

DENNIS. So why don't you ever sell any of that shit to pay *me*? You should let me call Adam Saulk's brother, man. He makes a fortune buying and selling that shit.

WARREN. I pay you.

DENNIS. You do not.

WARREN. Besides, paying you isn't like life and death. Anyway, you make so much money off all of us already it's like completely ridiculous.

DENNIS. Yeah, and I always smoke pot with you, all of you, *my* pot, all the time, like hundreds and hundreds of dollars' worth. So why shouldn't I make some money offa you? You fuckin' guys like *gripe* at me all the time, and I'm providing you schmucks with such a crucial service. Plus I'm developing valuable entrepreneurial skills for my *future*. *Plus* I'm like providing you with precious memories of your youth, for when you're fuckin' *old*. I'm like the basis of half your personality. All you do is imitate me. I turned you onto The *Honey*mooners, Frank *Zappa*, Ernst *Lubitsch*, *boxer* shorts,—*Sushi*. I'm like a one-man *youth* culture for you pathetic assholes. You're gonna remember your youth as like a gray stoned haze punctuated by a series of beatings from your dad, and like, *my* jokes. God *damn*. You know how much *pot* I've thrown out the *window* for you guys in the middle of the *night* when you're wandering around the street like *junkies* looking for half a *joint* so you can go to *sleep*, because you scraped all the *resin* out of your *pipes*? And you bitch about the fact that along the way I turn a little *profit*? You should thank God you ever *met* me, you little fuckin' hero-worshipping little *fag*.

WARREN. You are out of your mind, man.

> *Dennis laughs. Warren opens his big suitcase and starts removing the first items in an extensive collection of toys and memorabilia from the 1950s and '60s: Mint condition mid-'60s Mattel toys, first release albums, a 1950s toaster, etc.*

DENNIS. Don't take that stuff out in here.

WARREN. Why not? I wanna see what I can sell.

DENNIS. No—No—Don't take that stuff out in my apartment. It depresses me.

WARREN. Why?

DENNIS. Don't take all that cutesy kitschy retro-'60s bullshit out in my apartment. I don't wanna look at it.

WARREN. I can get a couple of hundred bucks for any of these albums.

DENNIS. Lemme see.

Warren hands him an obscure early Frank Zappa album.

Where'd you get this?

WARREN. From this buddy of mine in Seattle.

DENNIS. This is an amazing album.

Dennis looks through some of the stuff.

What is this shit? What's with the little *spacemen*? You are weird, man.

WARREN. This is Major Matt Mason. Don't you remember this?

DENNIS. No.

WARREN. They had these when we were little. They're really cool and these are in really good condition. I could get like a hundred fifty, two hundred bucks for this.

DENNIS. Seriously?

WARREN. Yeah.

DENNIS. So how do you always owe me money?

WARREN. 'Cause I don't wanna sell them.

DENNIS. You are a depressing little man. Now put that shit away.

WARREN. *(Holding it out to him.)* Look, he's got a little space helmet. The visor moves up and down.

DENNIS. Get that shit *away* from me!

The phone rings. Dennis answers on the second ring.

(Into the phone.) Yeah?… Because you're bein' a cunt.

The line goes dead. Dennis hangs up and laughs, suddenly energized.

WARREN. You're intense, man.

DENNIS. I'm the best! I don't let people freak me out. I freak *them* out.

WARREN. You're an amazing man.

DENNIS. Hey—Listen: That girl you like: what's her name?

WARREN. Jessica.

DENNIS. She's friends with that other girl, Natalie. You know her?

WARREN. Yeah?

DENNIS. OK, check it out: That girl Natalie likes me, OK? Last summer when Valerie was in Sweden with her family, I was like making out with her all the time, but that's all she ever let me do. But I saw her last week and she was coming onto me all over the place. So look: new plan: We'll take a thousand bucks out of the shoe bag, cab it over to Philip's house, pick up an ounce of blow, call Natalie, tell her and Jessica to come over here, we'll get them wired, I'll fuck Natalie—you do your best to fuck Jessica—Then tomorrow we make a few calls, sell the rest of the blow, turn a tidy little profit, and return the whole fifteen grand to your psychotic father intact on Monday. That's a great plan.

WARREN. How do you figure?

DENNIS. Because we extract a quarter ounce for ourselves, throw back in a quarter ounce of cut, sell it for like a hundred twenty-five a gram, clear around thirty-six hundred bucks, return the thousand dollar investment to the bag along with the two hundred you already owe him, and you're still gonna end up making like six hundred dollars.

WARREN. *(Slowly.)* ...All right...

DENNIS. OK?

WARREN. Yeah.

DENNIS. *(Grabbing the phone.)* OK—

WARREN. But like...what's the basic margin of profit?

DENNIS. Like eighteen hundred each.

WARREN. So but...if we're making eighteen hundred each, how come I only end up with *six*?

DENNIS. *(Still holding the phone.)* You *don't* end up with six: you end up with *eighteen*, minus the thousand you're investing and the two hundred you already *owe*. Plus a free eighth of blow. Which you can snort or sell as you see fit. Get it?

WARREN. Um, not really. But whatever.

DENNIS. What don't you get?

WARREN. I don't really get the whole thing.

Dennis hangs up the phone.

DENNIS. Look: We're buying a Z for a *thousand dollars...*

WARREN. No, I get *that* part. I just—I mean, theoretically, we're making a joint investment, right?

DENNIS. Yeah...?

WARREN. Only in terms of the actual cash outlay, it's all coming from my area. Right? So in a way, I'm the only actual investor.

DENNIS. Yeah...?

WARREN. So then why aren't I making all the money?

DENNIS. Because it's my connect and my customers and I'm gonna have the shit in my house.

WARREN. Yeah, but—

DENNIS. What do you *mean* why aren't you making all the money?

WARREN. I'm not saying I *should*. But you're saying we should split the profits *before* I put back the thousand dollars, and I'm saying like, why aren't we doing it *afterwards*?

DENNIS. Because it's my *connect*. I'm providing the *connect*.

WARREN. I'm providing the cash.

DENNIS. So what?

WARREN. ...So I figure the odds be fifty-fifty.

DENNIS. You do, huh? All right. Whatever... But that's fucked up, because I'm doing all the work, and all you did was steal some money from your father which you're getting back in like ten *minutes*.

WARREN. All right, so what do you want to do?

DENNIS. I don't know. I just—I should definitely get some kind of *service* fee. So look; we'll split the twenty six hundred net: thirteen hundred each. And then you pay me two hundred more for doing all the *work*—that leaves me with fifteen and you with eleven hundred. Out of which you can pay your father back the two hundred dollars or not. Whatever you want. OK?

WARREN. I guess.

DENNIS. Is that all *right* with you? Can I *call* him now?

WARREN. Yeah. Call him up.

DENNIS. Don't *ever* try to out-Jew me, little man. I'm twice the Jew you'll *ever* be. I'm like a Jewish *god*. I'm like—*Jooooo*lius *Caesar*!

WARREN. You're a fuckin' *mental* case, man.

DENNIS. Way to take care of *business*, little Warren!

> *Dennis pinches Warren very hard.*

WARREN. Ow!

> *Dennis dials the phone. Waits.*

DENNIS. *(To Warren.)* He's not there. *(Into the phone.)* Philly. Dennis. Call me. I'm looking for some fun.

> *He hangs up.*

Shit.

> *The phone rings. He lets it ring twice, then picks up.*

(Into the phone.) Yeah?... No... 'Cause I don't know... 'Cause I don't *give* a shit!... Yeah... Yeah, OK... *(To Warren.)* Go in the bathroom.

WARREN. Come on...

DENNIS. Go in the bathroom!

> *Warren goes in the bathroom.*

(Into the phone.) I'm sorry, baby. I know I messed up... I know! As soon as I start arguing I immediately snap into Attack Mode and just become as insanely brutal as I possibly can. It's because of my fucking *mother*... All right, why don't you come over?... Warren's here, but I'll get rid of him... Yeah... Oh, *really*?... No, totally *bring* her: Warren's like, in *love* with her... Would she be into that?... What if we got some blow?... She might. All right. See if she'll come over. I'll work on it.

> *He hangs up.*

Hey!

WARREN. *(Comes out of the bathroom.)* What's up?

DENNIS. Nothin'. I got good news for you, so get your little boner ready, 'cause my girlfriend's on her way over with your favorite teenage prostitute.

WARREN. What do you mean?

DENNIS. What do you think I mean?

WARREN. She's with Jessica?

DENNIS. Yeah.

WARREN. They're coming over here?

DENNIS. That's right, my little love machine.

WARREN. Excellent.

DENNIS. Only I told 'em we'd get drugs, so shut up for a second and let me think.

Pause. He picks up the phone and dials.

WARREN. Who are you calling?

Dennis ignores him.

DENNIS. *(Into the phone.)* Stuey. Hey. What are you doing?... You are too much, man. You shoulda been like, a Roman *Senator.* Let me ask you something: Have you seen this weed Christian's been selling? It's like an olive-colored dark green heavy sense with like a medium amount of fuzz, very wet and sticky, in like long oblong-shaped little buds, shaped like beef satay... Oh you got some?... Do you know where he got it?... All right: Let me ask you something else. Do you know where Philip is?... Yeah. Have you seen it?... How is it?... *Really.* How much did you get?... What's he asking?... I did. He's not home... No, I just *tried* him, you fat fuckin' pig, he's *not home.* Why do you have to aggravate me all the time?

WARREN. What's up?

DENNIS. *(Into the phone.)* So listen. Stuey. Baby: If I can't get ahold of Philip in like twenty, I'm comin' over there and taking an eighth offa you, all right?... No *Stuart,* I'm not *buying* it from you, I'm *taking* it, at cost. I'll give you cash up front, whatever you paid Philip, and you can get more from him tomorrow... *Yeah* as a *favor...* Because I'm *asking* you to, that's why. Because I *introduced* you to him in the first place, you fuckin' globulous *fuck.* You wouldn't even *know* him if it wasn't for me: you'd still be dealing commercial pot outside some Long Island mall to a bunch of dyed-blonde Great Neck *Bimbettes,* you fat fuckin' asshole. I *created* you, Stuey, and I can destroy you just as easily! I don't care how many syphilis-ridden Dutch backpackers are blowing you, man. Why do you always have to like, try to have some mincing little bullshit *advantage* over me all the time? So you don't feel like such a fat ugly *man* or something?… No, man, because you're like totally uncivilized. You have like no sense of protocol, like whatsoever… All right all right. I'll call you back.

> *He hangs up.*

WARREN. What's up?

DENNIS. Nothin'. He's sitting on his waterbed doing *speedballs* with some naked Dutch *hitchhiker* he picked up at the *bus* stop, and he wants to like *dicker* with me over the price of an eighth of coke, like I can't go over to Philip's myself tomorrow and pick it up for *less* than what *he* paid, and like I haven't turned him onto tons of business and tons of my own customers—just so he can be holding some kind of *cards* on me or something. Plus he's so stoned out of his mind to begin with you can't understand a word he's saying anyway.

WARREN. So…what are we gonna do?

DENNIS. I don't know. See if Philip calls back, and if he doesn't, we'll just have to deal with the Fat Man. Maybe we should just forget it. It's late anyway. I don't wanna be lying in bed grinding my teeth all night. Unless you wanna just stay up and watch *H.R. Pufnstuf* at 5:30 in the morning.

WARREN. I can't watch that show, man. It freaks me out.

DENNIS. All right. Should we get heroin? No, too much, right?

WARREN. Let's do speedballs.

DENNIS. Shut up. Do you even *know* what a speedball *is*? *No.*

WARREN. Yeah I know what a speedball is. It's like half heroin half cocaine. Right?

DENNIS. Yeah, but we can't give these girls *speedballs*. What are you, a maniac? Anyway, Valerie won't do heroin. *You* won't do heroin. So what are you talking about?

WARREN. I've done it.

DENNIS. Yeah, *once.* You'd be throwing up all night. That'd make a good impression. Speedballs are *sick*, man. They get you so fucked up you're like, really sorry.

WARREN. Let's do it!

DENNIS. Shut up.

Long pause.

WARREN. What's up?

DENNIS. No, nothing's *up*. How can you sit in a room with some-body for *hours* with nothing going on, and keep asking "What's up?" every ten minutes like something *new* happened all of a sudden that you didn't know about?

WARREN. I don't know. It's just an expression.

Warren is walking around the room, picking things up and looking at them.

So what's up? Where are they?

DENNIS. They're coming. Take it easy. And get away from my shit.

Warren keeps looking through Dennis' stuff.

WARREN. But do they know I'm here?

DENNIS. Yeah, yeah, I told 'em you're here, I totally set it up for you. Just don't get weird and bizarre and start talking about your dead sister, and you'll do fine.

WARREN. I'm not gonna talk about anything.

Pause.

DENNIS. Yeah, just don't be like—
I'm harsh?

WARREN. You're really harsh, man.

WARREN. Yeah.

DENNIS. Why? You should *face* that shit.

WARREN. I face it all the time.

DENNIS. Well why do you have like her childhood *pictures* up all over your room, and like articles about her *murder* in your fuckin' *drawer*, like ten years after the fact? You're gonna let that shit dominate your life? You gotta like, get *on* with it.

WARREN. I am getting on with it, man. That's why I have her picture up. So I can get on with it. She's fuckin' lucky she's dead anyway.

DENNIS. She is not. Shut up.

Pause. Dennis gets up and goes to his stereo and puts on a

record. It is a slow song, e.g., "Any Way the Wind Blows"*
from Ruben and the Jets. He holds out his arms and walks
toward Warren, singing along to him loudly.

WARREN. Get away from me.

> *Dennis keeps coming, looming over Warren, who tries to*
> *escape.*

Get away from me, man.

> *Dennis falls on top of him, crushing him with his body, still*
> *singing.*

Get off me, man!

> *Dennis laughs, screams. Warren struggles to get out from*
> *under him. Dennis gives him a loud wet kiss on the cheek*
> *and sits back. Warren pushes him over and sits up. Dennis*
> *flops onto his back. Warren walks around.*

DENNIS. I love Warren, man. He plays with me all day and all
night for as long as I want and he never complains.

> *He sits up, grabs the phone and dials.*

(Into the phone.) Stuey. It's me. I'm comin' over: What are you telling
me?… OK, *forget* it.

WARREN. What's up?

DENNIS. *(Covering the phone.)* He'll only sell us an ounce for
fifteen hundred if you give him the cash up front. So I'm not doing
that. I don't buy retail. But you can, if you want. But I'm not paying
this *pork* loin fifteen hundred bucks for an ounce of blow. It's not
worth my while.

WARREN. So let's—

DENNIS. *Unless*, we just keep an *eighth* for ourselves, instead of a
quarter. That way you still make your eleven hundred and I make
my fifteen. We just keep less blow for ourselves. *(Into the phone.)*
HOLD ON A SECOND! *(Covers the phone.)* So what do you want
to do?

WARREN. I'd go for it.

DENNIS. *(Into the phone.)* All right, I'm comin' over. Get dressed.

---

* See Special Note on Songs and Recordings on copyright page.

He hangs up and starts looking for his sneakers.

WARREN. So should we get some champagne or something?

DENNIS. All right. But I'm not payin' for that either.

WARREN. Nobody's asking you to.

DENNIS. What do you want, like Dom Pérignon?

WARREN. There is no other brand.

DENNIS. How many should I get? One bottle? Two?

WARREN. Let's get two.

DENNIS. They're expensive.

WARREN. That's no problem.

DENNIS. All right.

WARREN. So…how much do you need?

DENNIS. Gimme fifteen hundred for the blow and like two hundred for the champagne.

WARREN. The champagne's not gonna cost two hundred dollars.

DENNIS. Just gimme enough to cover it. Or let's just forget the whole thing. I don't wanna do any coke. It's a terrible drug. It's for chumps. It sucks. I'll fuck my girlfriend and go to sleep and you can go sleep in the park.

> *Pause. Warren goes to the shoe bag and starts counting out the money. Dennis starts putting on his sneakers.*

WARREN. So but…should I come with you, or what's the deal?

DENNIS. No, you gotta let Valerie in. She threw her key down the trash chute.

WARREN. No, man… I don't wanna deal with your girlfriend.

DENNIS. It's all right. We made up. Just stay here. I won't be long.

WARREN. Whatever.

> *Dennis finishes tying his sneakers and looks at him. Warren looks more nervous with every passing second.*

DENNIS. See—this is no good. You're already like freaked out and nervous. Forget it. That girl's gonna smell it the minute she comes in. What is the *matter* with you?

WARREN. What do you mean?

DENNIS. What are you, like, worried about what to *say*? Don't say *any*thing. Just sit there and look handsome, you Greek *god*. *She* should be worried about *you*. You're a handsome guy. You're like an intelligent fuckin' interesting guy. You don't have to *do* anything. Just don't get freaked out. We're gonna break this stupefying losing streak of yours wide open. Now gimme the money.

WARREN. All right. *(Pointedly.)* This is *seventeen hundred*.

DENNIS. *(Mocking his grave tone.)* "All right."

> *Dennis takes the money and shuffles into his coat.*

So just let 'em up and I'll be back in like twenty.

WARREN. Cool.

DENNIS. Be *glad*, man! She's really cute, she's got a great body and maybe you can actually fuck her.

WARREN. I'm gonna give it the old college try.

> *Dennis goes out. Warren locks the door after him. Steps back into the room, alone. He looks at himself in the mirror. He tries to make his appearance more casual, but it's a challenge. He untucks his shirt, musses his hair, etc. He finds the half-smoked joint, lights it and takes one huge hit. He sits there without moving. The buzzer buzzes. He gets up and presses the intercom button.*

Hello?

JESSICA. *(On the intercom.)* It's Jessica.

WARREN. OK.

> *Warren buzzes her in and moves away from the intercom. He checks his appearance one more time, then goes to the door and waits. There is a knock on the door. He waits for a second knock, then opens the door and steps back.*

You may enter.

> *Enter Jessica Goldman. She is the same age as Warren—around nineteen. She wears effective makeup, big shoes and a slightly pricey little dress that shows off her figure to good advantage. She is dressed up for the night, not down, and definitely looks a little out of place in Dennis' grunge palace. She is a very nervous girl, whose self-taught method of coping with her*

30

nervousness consists of seeking out the nearest available oasis of self-assurance and entrenching herself there with a watchful defensiveness that sweeps away anything that might threaten to dislodge her, including her own chances at happiness and the opportunity of gaining a wider perspective on the world that might eventually make her less nervous to begin with. Despite her prickliness she is basically friendly, definitely interested in Warren and trying to make a good impression.

JESSICA. Hi, Warren. How are you?

WARREN. I'm OK.

He hesitates, then leans in to kiss her hello, on the cheek. She is not expecting this, so it's a little physically embarrassing.

Um... Where's Valerie?

JESSICA. She went with Dennis. We ran into him downstairs and they said I should just come up.

She stands there, not sure where to go or what's appropriate.

WARREN. So how you doing, Jessica? You're looking very automated tonight.

JESSICA. What the fuck is *that* supposed to mean?

WARREN. Nothing. It's just a fashion concept.

JESSICA. What?

WARREN. Um—Nothing. You wanna come in?

She steps into the room.

JESSICA. So how long do you think they're gonna be?

WARREN. I don't know. Maybe a half hour?

JESSICA. What? What do you mean? Where do they have to go?

WARREN. Like, the East 50s.

JESSICA. Well... OK.

Pause.

I don't mean to be paranoid. I just don't want to be the victim of some teenage matchmaking scheme.

WARREN. Noted.

JESSICA. You know? If I'm gonna get set up, I'm gonna do it myself.

WARREN. Well nobody's setting you up, so why don't you calm down?

JESSICA. Oh you can't see why I would *think* that?

WARREN. I don't know or care what you think, Jessica. I'm just staying here because my *dad* threw me out of the *house*. But go home. It's fine with me.

JESSICA. *(Not an apology.)* OK, sorry.

> *She comes in.*

You probably think I'm like a total bitch now, right?

WARREN. I don't think anything. I don't even know what you're talking about.

> *He locks the door.*

And now…you're *mine*!

JESSICA. No *way*!

WARREN. I'm kidding! Calm *down*!

JESSICA. *(On "calm.")* That's not funny at *all*!

WARREN. *Noted.*

> *Jessica sits down and takes out her cigarettes and lighter.*

JESSICA. Is it OK if I smoke in here?

WARREN. Go ahead. It's not *my* house.

JESSICA. Well is there an ashtray or something I can use?

WARREN. I'm sure there's one somewhere.

> *He looks for an ashtray and finds one at the same time she finds an empty soda can.*

Here you go.

JESSICA. No, it's OK. I can use this. Thanks, though.

> *Warren puts down the ashtray and sits down across the room from her. She smokes. Long Silence.*

WARREN. So are you like a really big cigarette smoker?

JESSICA. I guess so.

WARREN. How many cigarettes would you say you smoke in the average day?

JESSICA. I don't know. Like a pack and a half a day, on a really heavy smoking day. Maybe like a half a pack a day if I'm like, in the country.

WARREN. ...Yeah... I never really got into the whole cigarette scene myself. But I hear great things about it.

JESSICA. Well, but if you smoke pot all the time it's much worse on your lungs than cigarettes.

WARREN. I guess my lungs are pretty severely damaged.

JESSICA. I'm sure they are.

> *Long silence.*

So did those guys go to get, um, to get coke?

WARREN. That's the plan.

JESSICA. I don't want to do very much.

WARREN. Well, we're getting like, a *lot.*

JESSICA. I'll do *some...*

WARREN. And we're getting some Dom Pérignon to top it off. So it should be pretty good.

JESSICA. Sounds good...

> *Long Silence.*

So why'd your dad throw you out of the house? What did you *do?*

WARREN. We just had a slight policy dispute. It's no big deal.

JESSICA. Are you staying here? Where are you gonna sleep?

WARREN. I don't know. It wasn't like a really detailed plan. I was just planning to crash on the floor for a few days till I figure out what I'm doing.

JESSICA. What *are* you gonna do?

WARREN. I don't know. I was thinking I might just buy a bus ticket and head out West. I have a buddy who lives in Seattle so I might just do that... I definitely wanna get out of *this—pit.* That's for sure.

JESSICA. You mean New York? You don't like living here?

WARREN. What's to like? You go outside and it *smells* bad. You know? And I live on Central Park *West.*

JESSICA. Well—

WARREN. I like the *out*doors.

JESSICA. I know, but—

WARREN. Like last winter I went to visit this buddy of mine who lives in Jackson Hole? In Wyoming? And we'd just *ski* every day, you know? And bus tables at night. And when you get up in the morning and open the front door it's like, *silent*. You know? You go outside and it's like, the *mountains*. And *snow*. And nobody around for *miles*. And like the whole...*sky* over your head. You know? So what the fuck am I doing languishing on *this* trash heap for? The intellectual stimulation? I'm not getting any. All I do is smoke pot. I can do that anywhere. I can just bring that *with* me, you know?

JESSICA. Yeah... I don't really take advantage of the city's facilities either, and it just seems like such a total waste.

WARREN. Yeah. I mean...yeah.

JESSICA. But—you're not planning on going to school at all? Didn't you *go* to school somewhere or something?

WARREN. Um, briefly.

JESSICA. So...?

WARREN. I... It just wasn't happening.

JESSICA. Where were you?

WARREN. Ohio.

JESSICA. Where, Oberlin?

WARREN. Whatever. You're at F.I.T., right?

JESSICA. Yeah. I really like it there. It's a little Jappy for me, but there's a lot of really great people there if you know where to look for them. But it's kind of weird, because I'm living at home—Which is great: like my mom and I get along incredibly well—but a lot of my formerly closest "friends" are out of the city now, and sometimes I wonder, you know, if I should've... I don't know.

WARREN. So are you heavily into fashion development?

JESSICA. Yeah. I've been doing a lot of designing. I've always done it. It's what I want to do.

WARREN. Well... My basic philosophy about clothes is that they should be comfortable, and not look like too many people had to slave over their creation. But then again, I'm not very fashion-oriented.

JESSICA. Yeah, but, you know, you will be someday.

WARREN. I doubt it.

JESSICA. Yeah, but you will. Your whole personality'll be different.

WARREN. You think?

JESSICA. Sure. What you're like now has nothing to do with what you're gonna *be* like. Like right now you're all like this rich little pot-smoking burnout rebel, but ten years from now you're gonna be like a plastic *surgeon* reminiscing about how wild you used to be…

WARREN. Well, I don't want to make any rash predictions at this point…but I seriously doubt I'm gonna be going in for plastic surgery.

JESSICA. Well, OK, whatever, but you'll definitely be a completely different person. Everything you think will be different, and the way you *act*, and all your most passionately held beliefs are all gonna be completely different, and it's really depressing.

WARREN. How do you figure?

JESSICA. Because it just basically invalidates whoever you are right *now*. You know what I mean? It just makes your whole self at any given point in your life seem so completely *dismissable*. So it's like, what is the point?

WARREN. I don't really know about that…

JESSICA. Well it's *true*.

WARREN. Maybe so, but I don't really *agree* with it.

JESSICA. Well, I've thought about this a lot.

WARREN. So have I.

JESSICA. I mean look who our *President* is now if you don't believe me.

WARREN. I'm not sure I follow you. But I guess—

JESSICA. No, like the classic *example* is all those kids from the '60s who were so righteous about changing the face of civilization, and then the minute they got older they were all like, "Actually, you know what? Maybe I'll just be a *lawyer*."

WARREN. I guess that's one interpretation…

JESSICA. But it's totally true! And now like Ronald *Reagan* is President of the United States. I mean, how embarrassing is *that*?

WARREN. It's pretty embarrassing… Although I have to say, I definitely know some people who are still seriously into civic activities. Like my mother does a fair amount of volunteer work for some kind of grape-picking civil liberties organization in California…

JESSICA. I know people who do that too. But I'm not talking about the last pathetic remnants of—Upper West Side Jewish…*Liberalism*. I'm talking about the *main*stream, and it is such a *joke*. I mean, I definitely feel that *evil* has like, triumphed in our time.

WARREN. So do *I*. But I still don't know if I would really ascribe all that to the theory that people's personalities undergo some kind of fundamental *alteration* when they get older.

JESSICA. Well, they do. And it's a big factor.

WARREN. I mean they obviously do to a *degree*—

JESSICA. Yeah!

WARREN. And things definitely happen to alter your general *trajectory*—

JESSICA. Yeah! And no matter—

WARREN. *(On "And.")* But I think that…you basically get a set of characteristics, and then they pretty much just develop in different ways. Like—

JESSICA. But can I just—

WARREN. *(On "can.")* Like the last year of high school, I suddenly realized that all these weird kids I grew up with were like well on their way to becoming really weird *adults*. And it was pretty *scary*, you know? Like you see a crazy kid, and you realize, he's never gonna grow *out* of it. He's a fucked-up crazy kid and he's just gonna be a fucked-up crazy adult with like a ruined life.

>   *Pause.*

JESSICA. Are you done now?

WARREN. I'm done with *that* thought.

JESSICA. Well can I please say something?

WARREN. Go ahead.

JESSICA. Thank you: I'm not saying anything about whether you're quote unquote "fucked up" or not. I don't mean it as a *moral* issue—

WARREN. Neither do I.

JESSICA. I just—

WARREN. *I* think that personality components are like protons and electrons. Like in science. Every molecule is made of the same basic components. Like the difference between a hydrogen molecule and a calcium molecule is like *one proton* or something…

JESSICA. Yeah? That's wrong, but yeah?

WARREN. So *my* theory is that people's *personalities* are basically constructed the same way. None of them are exactly the same, but they're all made of the same thing.

JESSICA. That's interesting.

WARREN. Thank you.

JESSICA. Unfortunately it has nothing to do with what I'm *talking* about.

WARREN. That is unfortunate.

JESSICA. I'm not talking about the chemical structure of your *brain*, I'm talking about—It's like, when you find an old *letter* you wrote, that you don't remember writing. And it's got all these thoughts and opinions in it that you don't remember having, and it's written to somebody you don't even remember having ever written a letter *to*.

WARREN. I've never found a letter like that.

JESSICA. Well I have. Like, a lot of them. And it just makes you realize that there's just these huge swaths of time in your life that didn't register at *all*, and that you might just as well have been *dead* during them for all the difference they make to you now.

WARREN. That seems like a fairly nihilistic viewpoint, Jessica.

JESSICA. Well, I am so completely the opposite of nihilistic it's amazing that anyone could even *say* that about me.

WARREN. Well—

JESSICA. BUT we don't agree. So that's OK. You think what you think and I think what I think, and there's no way we're ever going to convince each other, so my suggestion is we just drop it.

WARREN. All right.

Silence.

JESSICA. Hey, is there anything to drink in here? I've got this really bad taste in my mouth.

WARREN. *(Getting up.)* I think there's some water.

JESSICA. *(Starts to get up.)* I can get it.

WARREN. That's all right. "Chivalry is not dead. It just smells funny."

> *Jessica does not know how to respond to this, so she just looks at him. He gives up and goes the fridge, finds a juice jar full of cold water, pours some in a glass and brings it to her.*

JESSICA. Thanks a lot.

> *She takes the glass and drinks down the whole glass while Warren watches her.*

God, I was so thirsty.

> *Warren sits down, this time right next to her on the bed. He is sitting next to her, but not looking at her. It's making them both very nervous. Long silence. Jessica gets up and goes to the wall of photographs.*

So who are all these photos of? Are you on this wall?

WARREN. Yeah, I'm represented.

> *He follows her to the wall. She finds a photo with him in it.*

JESSICA. Wow, is this *you*?

WARREN. Yep.

JESSICA. God, what a little *stoner*. You look so different with long hair…

WARREN. Yeah. Everybody definitely went for the traditional post-high school chop.

JESSICA. Valerie says you just cut your hair when Dennis cut his hair.

> *Warren does not respond.*

Well, you definitely look better with it short.

WARREN. That seems to be the general consensus. But it makes me wanna like *instantly* have long hair.

> *Jessica scans the photographs.*

JESSICA. Wow. What a great picture of Dennis. I mean, he definitely has a slight cleanliness problem, but if he didn't, he'd be seriously gorgeous.

WARREN. You think?

JESSICA. Oh my God, are you *kidding*?

WARREN. I guess.

JESSICA. So his dad's like a really famous painter, right?

WARREN. I guess he's pretty famous.

JESSICA. Wow. So is that like, really hard for Dennis to deal with?

WARREN. I have no idea.

JESSICA. And his father's really sick or something?

WARREN. Uh… He's definitely having some pretty dire prostate problems.

JESSICA. His mom is beautiful…

WARREN. It's an incredibly attractive family.

JESSICA. What does she do?

WARREN. She's like a big city social worker administrator of some kind. She's always like installing swimming pools for the poor or something.

JESSICA. What?

WARREN. Nothing. She runs these programs for the city government or something. She designs social work programs for street kids and drug addicts and stuff like that. But she's a fuckin' psycho.

JESSICA. *(Bristling.)* Why do you say that? Just because she's a *social* worker?

WARREN. No—because of her behavior.

JESSICA. Why? What does she do?

WARREN. I don't know. She's just really *strident*. She's like a bleeding heart dominatrix with like a *hairdo*. She—

JESSICA. "Bleeding heart"?   WARREN. I don't know.

WARREN. Yeah!

JESSICA. What are you like a big Republican or something?

WARREN. Not at all. I'm a total *Democrat*. I just—

JESSICA. So why do you *say* that about her?

WARREN. Because that's what's she's *like*. But I don't really *care*. Maybe she's really nice. I don't really want to get into an argument about it.

JESSICA. No, it's just—My sister is a social worker, and I really—

WARREN. I didn't say anything *about* your sister.

JESSICA. I know you didn't. I just th—
I *know*—but I just think it's like a really good thing to do with your life and I j—OK, I *know*. I just admire people who dedicate themselves like that, and I—

WARREN. I didn't know you *had* a sister.

And I was not attempting to vilify the entire social worker *community*!

WARREN. So do *I*. What she *does* is fine. It's just how she *is*. I think it's totally brave to do that kind of work. Unless you're just—

JESSICA. Unless what?

WARREN. Unless you just have no sense of *people*. No—Like if your *mission* overrides your actual moral *opinion*, but—forget it. It's not—It doesn't matter.

JESSICA. All right. I certainly didn't mean to offend you.

WARREN. I'm not offended.

A moment. Jessica looks at the stuff in Warren's open suitcase.

JESSICA. Hey—what's this stuff?

WARREN. Those are just some of my belongings.

JESSICA. *(Looking through.)* What are these?

WARREN. It's just some fuckin' shit.

JESSICA. What are these, like antique toys or something?

WARREN. Um, for the most part…

JESSICA. These are really cool.

WARREN. You think?

JESSICA. Yeah, they remind me of the stuff my cousins had when I was a little kid. I always wanted to play with their toys and they were like, "Go play with dolls, you little bitch." And I was like "Fuck *you*!"… I *love* old toys.

40

WARREN. I have a fair amount of this kind of thing.

JESSICA. Do you know how many toys I had—I mean how much, of the stuff I had when I was little, I wish I had now? Like, I think of some of those toys and I just look back on them with this *longing*... You know?

WARREN. Definitely.

JESSICA. *(Takes out the Major Matt Masons.)* Who are these guys?

WARREN. That's my Major Matt Mason collection. You know Major Matt Mason?

She shakes her head.

Come on, Major Matt Mason, when we were kids—Aw, he's the *best*! Check him out, he's like, ready for his *mission*. I have a complete set, all in prime condition. I could actually sell them for a lot of money, but I'm hanging on to them.

JESSICA. Really cool.

WARREN. *(Shows her his heavy-duty 1950s toaster.)* And this is my amazing toaster. Toaster Amazing, I call it. Look at this. It's really something.

She looks.

Yeah, G.E. made only like a few hundred of this model like in the '50s, and then they recalled them because they were exploding in people's kitchens at breakfast and burning down their homes.

He laughs, sobers.

So only a few hundred actually exist. I got one from this dealer I know in Colorado and he had *no* idea what he was selling me.

JESSICA. Huh.

WARREN. I have made toast with it. But nothing bad happened to me. But I don't really use it too much because it really depreciates in value. But it's great to know I have one of the only ones in existence.

JESSICA. What's your favorite thing in this collection?

WARREN. Definitely my Wrigley Field Opening Day baseball cap my grandfather gave me. No contest.

JESSICA. What's that?

WARREN. *(Taking out an ancient blue and white baseball cap.)* This is a real collectors' item, like an *amazing* collectors' item, actually. My mom's dad got it the first day at Wrigley Field when he was totally like a little kid, in 1914.

JESSICA. *(Reads what's embroidered on the cap.)* "Wrigley Field, Home of the Chicago Cubs, Opening Day." *(Reads off the other side.)* "True Value."

WARREN. True Value Hardware, all right.

> *She puts the hat on.*

Looks good, Jessica...

> *She smiles. A moment.*

JESSICA. I didn't know your family was from Chicago.

WARREN. They're not. Just my grandfather. He was actually really cool. When he was a young man, he was like a fairly well-known aviator. You know, with like the fur-lined leather cap with the earflaps, and the whole bit. He actually set a couple of early endurance records in the nineteen twenties...

JESSICA. Wow... I didn't know that...

WARREN. Yeah...he was pretty interesting.

> *He laughs.*

Like whenever he would meet one of my friends, I'd be like, "Grampa, this is my friend Neil." And my grampa'd be like, "Nice to meet you, Neil. Are you Jewish?" And my friend Neil would be like, "Um... Yeah?" And my grampa'd be like, "Neil, in the year 1923 I was the greatest Jewish aviator in this country. That's because I was the *only* Jewish aviator in this country. You wanna see a picture?" And then he would break out his clippings which had these photos of himself in his fuckin' Sopwith Camel that he carried with him *all the time*. He was pretty amusing.

JESSICA. Is he still alive?

WARREN. Nah, nah...

JESSICA. Where does your mom live?

WARREN. Santa Barbara.

JESSICA. God, so why don't you go stay with her? That's supposed to be pretty nice.

WARREN. I don't particularly want to live in California, for one thing.

JESSICA. Why not?

WARREN. Because of the *people* in it. Plus my mom lives with her boyfriend... And anyway, she's kind of freaked out generally, so it's kind of tough to be around her for very long at one stretch.

JESSICA. Did you... Didn't you have a sister that died? Or something?

WARREN. Um...

>*He hesitates for a long moment.*

...Yeah. I did.

JESSICA. So—I mean—Is that why you say your mom, your mom is freaked out?

WARREN. I would say it was definitely a prominent factor.

JESSICA. What did your sister die of?

WARREN. Um, she was murdered.

JESSICA. Oh my God, is that true?

WARREN. No, that's just a little joke we have about it in the family.

JESSICA. What?

WARREN. Yeah it's *true.*

JESSICA. I'm sorry: I didn't mean, "Is that true?" I just meant... You know, "Oh my God."

WARREN. Yeah...

JESSICA. How did it happen? Do you mind talking about it...?

WARREN. Not really. Do you want any pot?

>*He picks up the roach.*

JESSICA. No, no thanks. But you go ahead.

WARREN. Um—That's all right.

>*He puts down the roach.*

JESSICA. So what happened? That is so horrible.

WARREN. Um, nothing. She was living with this guy named Julian. And my parents were kind of freaked out that she was living with this guy because she was only nineteen, and he was much older...

>*Very long pause.*

It's not really my favorite topic.

JESSICA. *(Blushing.)* I'm sorry...!

WARREN. That's OK...

JESSICA. ...I'm sorry.

WARREN. It's OK...

> *Long silence. She is very embarrassed. He holds out the roach to her.*

Do you want any of this?

JESSICA. OK.

> *He lights the roach and gives it to her. She takes a hit, doesn't get much, or coughs, but doesn't relight it or try again.*

The Wild City.

> *She looks at him thoughtfully for a moment.*

Are those your records?

WARREN. Um, yeah. These are my authentic first release '60s albums, all in perfect condition. Got the whole thing here: Early Mothers, Captain Beefheart, Herman's Hermits, everything. You wanna hear one?

JESSICA. Sure.

> *He puts on a high-velocity Frank Zappa song, e.g., "Mystery Roach"* from* 200 Motels.

All right!

> *She nods and starts dancing.*

Wake this dump *up!*

WARREN. All right.

> *Warren starts dancing in his own separate space. He takes a few tentative steps toward her, then she moves unambiguously to him and they start dancing more or less together.*

JESSICA. Uh *huh*, uh *huh*, uh *huh* uh *huh* uh *huh*.

> *She opens her arms and Warren steps into them. The music abruptly ends with a Zappa-esque confusion of sound and becomes something weird and impossible to dance to.*

---

* See Special Note on Songs and Recordings on copyright page.

WARREN. Um—I don't know. I guess you can't really dance to this next song too well.

JESSICA. Well…

WARREN. Hold on.

He hurries to the stereo and puts on a slow, romantic song.

JESSICA. Oh. OK. Goes for the slow song. I get it.

WARREN. Of course.

JESSICA. OK. I'm game.

She starts to take his hands.

Wait.

She lets go.

I've got a hair in my mouth.

She extracts the hair from her mouth, shakes it off her finger and puts her hands back up. They dance, not entirely gracelessly.

WARREN. I'm definitely into actual dancing.

JESSICA. Yeah, I think our generation definitely missed out in the dancing department.

WARREN. Yeah… I guess like, whoever the genius was who decided you didn't need *steps* should have come up with something else instead.

JESSICA. Yeah, right?

He dips her.

Check him out. Mr. *Dip.*

He brings her back up again.

You could be a really good dancer.

WARREN. Thanks. So could you. *(A joke.)* If only society would give us a chance.

JESSICA. Yeah, man!

They dance.

WARREN. Listen—

JESSICA. Yeah?

WARREN. I just gotta say, I find you incredibly attractive.

JESSICA. OK—Relax, will you?

WARREN. But listen—Would you be mortally offended if I kissed you for just a second?

JESSICA. Well, I mean, what's the rush?

WARREN. No rush. I'd just like to get rid of this knot in my stomach.

JESSICA. Oh—Sure, I mean—Whatever's expedient.

WARREN. *(Moving closer.)* No—It's just…

JESSICA. *(Letting him.)* Yeah…?

> *Warren kisses her. She kisses back. It quickly turns into heavy teenage-style making-out. Jessica breaks away.*

They're gonna walk in and I'm gonna be really embarrassed.

WARREN. *(A blatant lie.)* Yeah—me too.

> *She takes a few steps away and looks back at him sharply.*

JESSICA. They *are* coming back, right?

WARREN. Yeah…!

JESSICA. OK. Just checking.

> *Pause.*

But I mean…do you like me, Warren, or what?

WARREN. Of course I do. Can't you tell?

JESSICA. I don't know. Not really. Maybe you just want to mess around or something.

WARREN. Um, I do. *And* I like you. And I completely enjoy talking to you…

JESSICA. Well, OK. Which would you prefer if you had to choose?

> *Pause.*

WARREN. That would depend on which one we'd already been doing more *of.*

JESSICA. All right. Never mind. Stupid question. I'm sorry: It's just, I'm always getting drawn into these situations and then getting hurt really badly. So…

WARREN. Noted.

JESSICA. You wanna close your eyes for a second?

WARREN. Yes.

> *He closes his eyes. Jessica crosses to him and kisses him, until they are both sprawled inelegantly on Dennis' horrible mattress, feeling each other up and getting so worked up that Jessica pulls away again, not out of coquetry but just to put on the brakes.*

JESSICA. OK, gotta take a break.

WARREN. Well… I mean—If you want to, we could go someplace else.

JESSICA. What do you mean? Like, to your house or something?

WARREN. Um—No, my house wouldn't work out too well right now…

JESSICA. Well, we can't go to *my* house.

WARREN. Well, look, why don't we—Why don't we just go rent the Penthouse Suite at the *Plaza*, and like hang out and order room service and like watch the sun come up over the Park.

JESSICA. How could we do that?

WARREN. I happen to be extremely liquid at the moment.

JESSICA. Are you serious?

WARREN. Yeah—!

JESSICA. Well…what about Dennis and Valerie?

WARREN. I'll leave them a note. Or, we can just tell them where we are, and have them meet us there, or we can just hang out by ourselves… Whatever we feel like doing.

JESSICA. Um—All right.

WARREN. Really?

JESSICA. Sure. I mean… Yeah.

WARREN. All right. Let me just get some funding.

> *He goes to the shoe bag and takes out a couple of bricks of cash.*

JESSICA. Oh my *God*. Is that *money* in there?

WARREN. I'm afraid so.

JESSICA. Where did you get that?

WARREN. These are the proceeds from my unhappy childhood.

JESSICA. The what…?

WARREN. I'll tell you about it later. Are you ready?

JESSICA. I'm ready.

> *She slings her purse over her shoulder. Stops.*

Shit! I should've called my mother.

WARREN. What for?

JESSICA. I'm just supposed to call her if I'm gonna be out after twelve-thirty.

WARREN. Doesn't that wake her?

JESSICA. She doesn't care, she just goes back to sleep.

WARREN. Do you want to call her now?

JESSICA. No. She's just gonna freak out 'cause I didn't call earlier. I don't know. I'll just deal with it later… *(As they head for the door.)* I don't know why the fuck she's always so worried about me.

> *Warren shrugs. They go out.*

End of Act One

ACT TWO

The next day, a little after noon. On the little table is a small laboratory scale, a brown paper bag, an unopened jar of mannitol, a tablespoon, an upside-down porcelain dinner plate, a nearly unfurled ten-dollar bill, and a straight-edged razor. Dennis is sprawled out asleep on his mattress in a crazy tangle of sheets, wearing only a T-shirt and a pair of boxer shorts. The buzzer buzzes. Dennis stirs but does not wake. The buzzer buzzes again. He sits up, then staggers to the intercom and presses the talk button.

DENNIS. *What?*

WARREN. *(On the intercom.)* It's Warren!

Dennis buzzes him in, unlocks the door and leaves it ajar, then collapses back onto the bed. Warren comes in, looking chipper. He carries a small deli bag with a coffee in it.

Hey.

DENNIS. Where've you been? What happened to you?

WARREN. Nothing. I was with Jessica.

DENNIS. You were with her this whole time?

WARREN. Pretty much.

DENNIS. What time is it?

WARREN. Around noon.

Dennis goes into the bathroom, leaving the door open. We hear him pee and flush the toilet. He comes out.

So… Did you get that Z from Stuey?

DENNIS. Yeah. It's *great.* Me and Valerie were doing lines with him and *Bergita* for like two and a half hours. Plus he says the heroin he has is like really amazing too.

WARREN. Who's Bergita? The Dutch girl?

DENNIS. Yeah. She was pretty cute. I don't understand how this guy gets girls, man. He is like a classically ugly man.

He collapses on the bed again.

WARREN. Where's Valerie?

DENNIS. Oh, *Valerie.* Valerie walked in here and took one look at the shards of her *sculpture* lying in the garbage and went completely insane. She was screaming at me so loud it literally hurt my *ears.* She was like, "You're totally selfish, you do whatever you want, you never apologize to anyone, you have no idea how to deal with people, and you're gonna die alone." Then she burst into tears and fled to her aunt's house in Connecticut. I totally blame you.

WARREN. Sorry about that, man.

DENNIS. I don't give a shit. She's out of her mind.

WARREN. So—is this it?

DENNIS. Yeah.

> *Warren picks up a brown paper bag off the table and very carefully takes out of it a double-wrapped ziplock baggy containing an ounce of cocaine.*

WARREN. That's a lot of blow.

DENNIS. Yeah. Now put it down before you *break* it.

> *Warren puts down the bag of cocaine.*

So what happened with you and that girl?

WARREN. Nothing. I had a nice time.

DENNIS. Did you fuck her?

WARREN. Um… Yeah. I did.

DENNIS. You *did*? As in actual penetration?

WARREN. Basically.

DENNIS. No—what do you mean "basically"? Did you or didn't you?

WARREN. No—I did.

DENNIS. So that's amazing.

WARREN. I'm pretty pleased.

DENNIS. *Warren.* Breaks the losing streak.

WARREN. Yeah. I kind of like her. She really likes to argue. But I'm into that.

DENNIS. So where did you go? Her house?

WARREN. No, man, I took her to the fuckin' Vanderbilt Suite at the Plaza *Hotel*.

DENNIS. No you didn't.

WARREN. Yes I did.

DENNIS. You took her to the *Plaza*?

WARREN. Yeah. I got this really beautiful suite and we just drank champagne and looked out over the Park and made love on the balcony. It was pretty intense.

Pause.

DENNIS. You should have gone to the Pierre.

WARREN. Why do you say that?

DENNIS. Because the Plaza is a dump. My old man says it used to be amazing, but it's totally run down and rancid now and the Pierre is just a much, much better hotel. You gotta stay at the Pierre or the Carlton or like the Carlyle.

WARREN. Well—I never stayed at any of them, but I definitely thought the Plaza was pretty cool.

DENNIS. So were you actually able to do anything with her? Or did you just like come immediately?

WARREN. I came pretty fast.

DENNIS. Naturally. You only did it once?

WARREN. Well… I think she kind of freaked out a little bit afterwards.

DENNIS. What do you mean? What'd she do?

WARREN. Well, she didn't really freak *out*, but she definitely got pretty quiet. And I was like, "What's the matter? We just had an amazing time together and I really like you." And she was like, "But I don't even *know* you." So I was like, "Well you know me *now*." But I don't really know if she agreed with that interpretation.

> *Dennis crosses to the table and starts opening up the bag of cocaine to show Warren.*

DENNIS. Yeah. Don't worry about that. A lot of times your average girl teen will bug out immediately following a swift and manly conquest. It's no big deal. You didn't do anything to her that she didn't do to you. Just call her up and, you know, take her to the *zoo* or something. Only don't sit here and start getting depressed after you finally got laid with a completely good-looking girl after a *draught* like the fucking Irish *potato* famine of *1848*, because you're bringing me down. You should be totally proud of yourself and not get into your usual self-flagellating stew just because you came too fast and she freaked out afterwards.

> *He laughs.*

Now come here and take a look at the crystal formation on this rock. It's unbelievable.

WARREN. *(Looks.)* That's a big rock.

DENNIS. It's a big rock. This baby alone would probably pay for your whole *night* at the Plaza. You know?

WARREN. I doubt it.

DENNIS. Why? How much did you spend?

WARREN. I haven't really tallied it up yet, but I guess it was about a thousand bills, all told.

DENNIS. You spent a *thousand dollars* on that girl when she was totally ready to fuck you for free?

WARREN. I wasn't so sure, man. She seemed kinda skittish.

DENNIS. So, what, now you're in the hole for twenty-five hundred bucks?

WARREN. Twenty-seven.

DENNIS. What is the *matter* with you? How did you spend that much *money*?!?

WARREN. I'm not really sure.

DENNIS. OK: You're outta control! You are like hell bent for destruction and I want nothing more to fuckin' do with it! I can't sell twenty-seven hundred dollars worth of blow before tomorrow *morning*.

WARREN. Why not?

DENNIS. Because it's totally impossible! I'll make the *calls*, but I can't speed the natural pace of the market. It's just not gonna happen. Besides, your share of the profits only comes to thirteen hundred minus my service fee! And even if it *didn't*, I'm not letting you stay here all week with that money, Warren, because when your father finds out you spent that money on drugs, he's gonna think I'm in *cahoots* with you, and then he's gonna forgive *you* and kill *me*.

WARREN. No he's not.

DENNIS. Yes he is! How could you spend another thousand dollars?!

WARREN. It was surprisingly easy.

DENNIS. All right: That's it. Get on the phone, call Christian, tell him we need distribution help. Tell him you'll give him whatever he wants out of your half and if he can't help us move all 20 grams by tonight you're comin' over there to stay with him. Because I am officially closing the Dennis Ziegler Home For Runaway Boys. You understand me?

WARREN. Who am I calling? Christian?

DENNIS. Yeah, Christian!

WARREN. All right...!

As Warren picks up the phone Dennis roams around the room.

DENNIS. Oh you are so stupid, man. You are so stupid. If your father finds you here, man, he's gonna sic that fuckin' *driver* on me and I am totally gonna have to leave town. And this is such a bad time for me.

WARREN. *(Holding the phone.)* Did you have breakfast yet?

DENNIS. No I didn't have breakfast. I just got up.

WARREN. Let's take a run over to Zabar's and pick up a smoked salmon.

DENNIS. DIAL THE PHONE!

Warren dials the phone.

WARREN. *(Into the phone.)* Hello Mr. Berkman, is Christian there?... Oh, OK. Could you please tell him that Warren Straub called?... I'm fine, how are you?... Not too much. How's *Mrs.* Berkman?

DENNIS. Get off the phone!

WARREN. *(Into the phone.)* Anyway—could you just tell him I called and he can call me at Dennis Ziegler's house?

Dennis makes a wild negative cut-off gesture.

Actually, just tell him I'll try him later... Thanks a lot.

He hangs up.

DENNIS. What's the *matter* with you?

WARREN. Nothing. Why don't you calm down?

DENNIS. Oh you are really asking for it. Maybe I can get ahold of Philip.

> *The phone rings. They look at it fearfully. It keeps ringing. Dennis picks it up tentatively.*

(Into the phone.) Yeah?... BECAUSE *I* DIDN'T BREAK YOUR FUCKING SCULPTURE, *WARREN* BROKE IT!!!

> *He slams the phone down as hard as he possibly can. Runs his raging fingers through his hair. Warren starts to speak—Dennis grabs the phone and dials furiously. Waits.*

(Into the phone.) I just want you to think about what a sick, unhappy person you are that after all the serious problems we've been having for the last three months over your relentless *identity* crisis—*which has nothing to fucking do with me!*—we're finally getting along together like we fuckin' love each other, and you freak out at me *this much* and get me *this angry* at you, because one of my *friends* accidentally broke your semi-Lesbian Progressive School clay *sculpture*?... It was on the *shelf* so I could *look* at it! Will you *listen* to yourself? Will you listen to what you're *saying*?... YOU TORTURE ME ABOUT A SCULPTURE, YOU PSYCHOTIC MONSTER!? I'D LIKE TO RIP YOUR FUCKIN' HEAD OFF!

> *He slams the phone down and kicks it as hard as he can across the room. Pause.*

WARREN. You have a nice touch, man.

DENNIS. Shut up!

> *He starts laughing.*

I'm sick, *sick*! All right: Christian's not home and I ain't callin' Philip. What about this shit? Could you sell any of this?

> *He rattles Warren's open suitcase full of toys.*

WARREN. Um—Yeah. I can sell *all* of it.

DENNIS. Really? For how much? Could you get two thousand dollars for what's in here?

WARREN. I don't know. I never really tallied it up, but I'm fairly sure I could get considerably *more* than that.

DENNIS. Oh, we are selling this *today*. I'm calling Adam Saulk's brother right now.

He picks up the phone. Stops.

Is that OK?

WARREN. Go ahead.

Dennis dials the phone.

DENNIS. All right. Maybe this'll solve everything. *(Into the phone.)* Is that Donald?... Dennis Ziegler, man, what's goin' on?... I'm all right. Listen, do you know Warren *Straub*?... Yeah. So he's got like a lot of really high quality toys and shit from like the '50s and '60s, and about thirty really rare first release albums— *(Covers the phone. To Warren, who is signalling him.)* What?

WARREN. I think you should mention the toaster.

DENNIS. No, he doesn't care about your *toaster*, Warren. *(Into the phone.)* One second, man.

WARREN. Yes he does. It's really rare.

DENNIS. *(Covers the phone.)* It's worth money?

WARREN. *Yeah.*

DENNIS. *(Into the phone.)* Sorry, man—He's also got this incredibly rare toaster from like... Eighteen-forty-*seven*.

WARREN. Nineteen-fifty-five.

DENNIS. *(Into the phone.)* From nineteen-fifty-*five*. Like a completely rare edition of toaster. I'm not sure what the actual model is, but—I said I'm not sure what the actual *model* is, but I definitely know it is one fine toaster. *(Covers the phone.)* Would you shut up?!

WARREN. Tell him they recalled it.

Tell him they recalled it.

D. Tell him they recalled it!

Warren shuts up.

DENNIS. *(Into the phone.)* Yeah, man—anyway—he was gonna sell some of this shit to his regular boy, but I told him I had a friend who could probably come up with a much better price, and I wanted to try to give you the business if you were interested. But the thing is, Donald? Donald? This stuff is like really good, so I don't wanna waste my time if you're not totally prepared to step up to the plate. You know what I mean there, Donald?... Yeah? All right... No, this afternoon's not so good for me, man, I'm going to a ball game with my brother... No, man, Warren's like ready to *go*... Well what are you doing right now?... All right, gimme your address.

> *He writes down the address.*

All right, man, see you in a few.

> *He hangs up.*

I am a total business *genius*. I don't even know what this shit is *worth* and I'm already getting you like the best possible price for it. I am just like completely naturally gifted at business.

WARREN. Well... There is my usual guy, who's definitely offered me decent money for the whole collection at various times, so—

DENNIS. No, never mind your usual *guy*. You should totally let me handle this transaction for you, Warren, because this guy is like completely intimidated by me and I'm just gonna get you much more money. All right?

WARREN. Whatever.

DENNIS. All right. Now before I go over there, tell me what would be the best possible money you could *possibly* get for this shit.

WARREN. I don't know. If you include the records, I guess the best price you could hope to get would be like, I don't know, like maybe twenty-five at the very outside.

DENNIS. You're seriously telling me this *junk* is worth twenty-five hundred bucks?

WARREN. Yeah. Because it's a really good collection. But you probably won't get that.

DENNIS. All right. Now listen, Warren. I am not selling your *baby* toys if you don't tell me it's OK. Because I don't want you *guilting* it over my head for the rest of my life. OK? But if you *don't* want me to, I am totally throwing you out of here right now. Because I have no desire to incur the Wrath of *Jason*, and you can't just walk in here and dump your *situation* on me and then obstruct every possible solution I come up with, just because you're a destructive little *freak* who has to like *wreck* everything so you can get everybody whipped into a *frenzy* over you all the time. But I don't want you telling me later that I forced you into selling your precious belongings, because it's totally up to *you*. All right?

WARREN. No. Go ahead and sell 'em. I don't know what else to do.

> *Dennis starts getting dressed.*

DENNIS. All right. If this stuff is worth twenty-five bills then I probably won't have to sell *all* of it, so tell me which of these I should try to hang on to and which I should immediately toss into the gaping maw of Donald Saulk.

WARREN. I guess…save the Major Matt Masons for last… And if you can, I guess I'd prefer it if you didn't sell the toaster.

> *Pause.*

DENNIS. I just totally humiliated myself talking *up* this fucking toaster, now you're telling me I can't *sell* it?

WARREN. Not if you don't have to, no. *I* don't know how much he's gonna offer—

DENNIS. All right. I'll try.

WARREN. And give me the hat.

DENNIS. *(Picks up the baseball cap.)* We can't sell this?

WARREN. I don't think so.

DENNIS. Why not? You could get money for this, couldn't you?

WARREN. I know I could, but I'm not selling it.

DENNIS. All right.

> *Dennis gives Warren the baseball cap and starts packing up the suitcase. The buzzer buzzes.*

It's Jason!

WARREN. It's not Jason!

DENNIS. It's totally Jason. I'm going across the roof!

WARREN. It's not Jason, he doesn't even know I'm here!

DENNIS. He knows who your *friends* are!

WARREN. But it's not *him*, you fuckin' *socio*path: he's throwing a *brunch*!

DENNIS. You think he didn't figure out where you *went*? You only *have* two friends! All *right*!

>*Pause.*

DENNIS. You answer it.

WARREN. No way.

DENNIS. Why not?

WARREN. Because it's not my house, man.

DENNIS. So what?

WARREN. I don't wanna answer it. What if it's him?

DENNIS. All right. Shut up.

WARREN. I wasn't talking.

DENNIS. Shut up!

>*Dennis goes to the intercom and hits the talk button.*

Yeah?

JESSICA. *(On the intercom.)* It's Jessica Goldman. Is Warren there?

DENNIS. *(To Warren.)* I'm gonna *kill* you, Warren.

WARREN. I didn't know she was coming here.

DENNIS. That scared the shit out of me.

WARREN. Why? Just buzz her in.

>*Dennis hits the buzzer and goes to the suitcase.*

DENNIS. All right. Saulk's only on 81st, so I won't be long. I'll do my best and I'll try to save Major Matt Mason if I can. But he might be called upon to make the ultimate Outer Space sacrifice.

WARREN. I understand, man… Farewell, Toaster Amazing.

>*Warren unhappily watches Dennis pack away the last of the collection and zip up the suitcase.*

DENNIS. All right. Cheer up, man. Your troubles are almost over.

WARREN. I'm cheerful.

>*There is a knock on the door. Dennis is nearest the door and opens it. Jessica stands in the doorway.*

JESSICA. Hi, Dennis. How are you?

DENNIS. I'm fine, Jessica. How are *you?*

JESSICA. Fine.

DENNIS. Are you from the Leg Embassy?

He is referring to her short skirt.

JESSICA. Yeah, I'm the Ambassador.

DENNIS. Stay with it.

JESSICA. *(Comes into the room. To Warren.)* Hey. I was just around the corner so I thought I'd buzz up.

WARREN. *(Bizarrely, to Jessica.)* Good Morgen to all good Norsemen.

JESSICA. Excuse me?

WARREN. How many Norse Horsemen does it take to Smoke a Herring?

> *Dennis laughs rudely and loudly at Warren's awkward attempt at eccentric humor and goes into the bathroom, closing the door behind him. We hear the sink running. Warren crosses with awkward confidence toward Jessica.*

All Norse Horsemen smoke Morgen Cigarettes.

JESSICA. Am I supposed to know what you're talking about?

WARREN. I'm not talking about anything. It's just something to say. Don't you want to kiss me Good Morgen?

> *He comes to her to kiss her. It doesn't go too well. She turns her face or ducks her head so he can't kiss her.*

JESSICA. *(Low, referring to Dennis in the bathroom.)* Um, can we please not, like…

WARREN. Sorry.

JESSICA. That's OK…

> *She moves away from him. Dennis comes out of the bathroom. He sits on the floor to put on his sneakers.*

WARREN. So D. How long you think you're gonna be?

DENNIS. *(Looking at Jessica.)* I don't know. How much time do you need?

WARREN. *(Confused.)* Um… We were gonna get some food…

JESSICA. How much *time* do we need?

DENNIS. *(To Warren.)* So who's stoppin' you?

WARREN. I was actually wondering about the *key*.

JESSICA. *(To Dennis.)* How much time do we need for *what*?

DENNIS. For whatever dastardly deed you're planning to *indulge* in, Jessica.

JESSICA. I don't think we're gonna be indulging in anything very dastardly, to tell you the truth, Dennis.

WARREN. I thought we were gonna be indulging in some *brunch*.

DENNIS. So *that's* your story, eh? *(À la Snidely Whiplash.)* Yeh heh heh heh…!

JESSICA. What is he *talking* about?

WARREN. Denny, man, you're my *best friend*.

DENNIS. *(Getting up.)* All right, kids, I'm outta here. Try to find some way to entertain yourselves.

JESSICA. Don't leave on my account.

DENNIS. Don't worry about it. *(To Warren.)* Be back in a half.

Dennis exits, with the suitcase.

JESSICA. Where's he going?

WARREN. He just has a business transaction to perform.

JESSICA. What is he, like the big drug dealer or something?

WARREN. He's the big everything.

JESSICA. Well… Sorry to bust in on you like this—

WARREN. That's OK.

JESSICA. —but I actually just wanted to tell you I can't have brunch.

WARREN. Why not?

JESSICA. Well, when I got home this morning I got into this really huge fight with my mom and I think I'd better just be at home today. She kind of freaked out that I never called last night, so now she wants to have some big Landmark Discussion about how we're gonna handle my *living* there this year…

WARREN. Well… Thanks for cancelling in person.

JESSICA. Well, I'm sorry, but my mom's really upset and getting along with her is a really big priority for me right now. I tried to call before, but the line was busy.

WARREN. Do you want to make a plan for any time this week?

JESSICA. I think I'd better just chill out a little bit this week, actually.

WARREN. All right.

    Silence.

JESSICA. Well... You seem like you're really angry...

WARREN. I'm not.

JESSICA. Well, that's not the impression you're *conveying*, but...

WARREN. No—I guess I just don't understand why you walked ten blocks out of your way so you could be around the corner so you could buzz up and tell me you can't have brunch with me.

JESSICA. Uh, *no:* I told you I tried to call...

WARREN. Yeah—he was on the phone for like two minutes.

JESSICA. All right, I'm *sorry.*

WARREN. There's nothing to be sorry about.

JESSICA. All right.

    She goes slowly to the door and puts her hand on the knob.

So...can I ask you something?

WARREN. Go ahead.

JESSICA. Did you tell Dennis what happened last night?

    Pause.

WARREN. Um...I guess.

JESSICA. Really. What did you say?

WARREN. Nothing. I said we had a nice time.

JESSICA. That's all?

WARREN. Pretty much.

JESSICA. I find that really hard to believe.

WARREN. Why?

JESSICA. I don't know. Don't you guys get into like, comparing notes and stuff?

WARREN. I'm not really into that.

JESSICA. Well…OK… It's just—This is getting a little weird now, because when I talked to Valerie, she asked *me* if anything happened with us last night, and for some reason, I guess I didn't really tell her that anything did. So now she's gonna talk to *Dennis* and I'm gonna look like a total *liar* to someone I'm just starting to be close friends with and who I really care about…!

WARREN. Um… So… I don't really get… You're mad at me because you lied to Valerie?

JESSICA. No, I just should have figured that you would like rush off to tell your friends that you *fucked* me—

WARREN. Whoa!

JESSICA. —whereas I might be more inclined to be a little more *discreet* about it till I found out where I *stood* with you.

WARREN. I didn't fuckin' rush off *anywhere*!

JESSICA. Yeah, whatever, you know what? It doesn't matter—

WARREN. I came *back* here 'cause I'm *staying* here—

JESSICA. OK, but you know what? It really doesn't matter—

WARREN. And the minute I walked through the door he like totally *grilled* me—

JESSICA. Oh so you just tell him anything he wants to know no matter what the consequences are for somebody else?!

WARREN. No! Will you let me finish my—

JESSICA. *(On "Let.")* But honestly, Warren? I really don't care who you told, or what you told them, because people are gonna think whatever they think and you know what? There's nothing I can do about it.

WARREN. What people? What are you talking about!?

JESSICA. I don't know, but whatever it is I must be wrong because of the way you're *yelling.*

WARREN. You're not anything!

JESSICA. Well, it really—I should just really listen to my instincts, you know? Because your instincts are never wrong. And it was totally against my instinct to come over here last night, and it was definitely against my instinct to *sleep* with you, but I did and it's too late. And now my mom is totally furious at me, I probably ruined my friendship with Valerie, and now like Dennis *Ziegler* thinks I'm like, easy *pickins*, or something—!

WARREN. Nobody thinks *anything*—

JESSICA. And it's not like I even care what he thinks, OK? Because I don't actually *know* him. Or you. Or *Valerie*, for that matter! So it doesn't really matter! I've made new friends before, I can make more new friends now if I have to. So let's just forget the whole thing ever happened, you can chalk one up in your *book*, or whatever—

WARREN. I don't *have* a book.

JESSICA. —and I'll just *know* better next time! Hopefully. OK?

      Pause.

WARREN. I don't really get what you're so upset about.

JESSICA. Well: I guess I'm just *insane.*

WARREN. I thought we had a really good time together, and I was actually in a fairly Up state of mind for once.

JESSICA. I'm sure you were.

WARREN. Well, I didn't mean that in any kind of lascivious way, so I don't know why you want to take it like that. I really like you.

JESSICA. Yeah, whatever.

WARREN. No not whatever! I'm sorry I said anything to Dennis. I definitely caved in to the peer pressure. But I also definitely said as little as possible and was totally respectful of you in the way I talked about you. Even though I was pretty excited about what happened last night, and also about like, maybe like, the prospect of like, I don't know, like, going *out* with you—Which I would be very into, if you were. But if you want to think the whole thing meant nothing to me, then go ahead, because that's not the case.

JESSICA. Well… You know, I really—

WARREN. It's totally weird, like taking all your clothes off and having sex with someone you barely know, and then being like, "What's up *now*?" You know? Like it's such an intense experience, but then nobody knows what to fuckin' say, even though nothing really bad actually happened. You know?

JESSICA. …Well…I don't know…

WARREN. But I really like you… I don't really agree with most of your *opinions*…

JESSICA. Oh, thank you.

WARREN. …but I don't meet a lot of people who can actually make me *think*, you know? And who can hold their own in an interesting discussion. And who I'm totally hot for at the same time. You know? It's a fairly effective combination.

    Pause.

JESSICA. I don't know, Warren. Things are just really weird in my life right now. And everything you're saying is really sweet, but I have literally no idea whether you mean it or not. It's like my instinct is just *broken*… And I guess sometimes actions speak louder than words…

WARREN. But what action could I possibly take except to say that I'm sorry for whatever it is you think I've done?

JESSICA. *(A joke.)* Presents are always nice. Just kidding.

WARREN. You want a present?

JESSICA. I'm just kidding.

WARREN. Why? I'm sitting on twelve thousand *dollars*. I'll buy you a *sports* car. OK?

JESSICA. That's OK. I don't even have a license yet.

WARREN. Well, what do you want?

    Pause.

JESSICA. …Are you serious?

WARREN. *Name* it.

JESSICA. OK…

    Pause. She looks around the room. Her eyes light on the baseball cap.

Um… Could I have the hat?

    Pause.

WARREN. Definitely.

    Pause.

JESSICA. Really?

WARREN. It's yours.

He picks up the baseball cap and holds it out to her.

Here.

JESSICA. *(Looks at him uncertainly.)* …Don't if you don't want to.

WARREN. I really want to.

JESSICA. Why?

WARREN. Because I really like you.

> *Pause. She reaches out slowly and takes the hat.*

JESSICA. Well—I don't know what to say…

> *Warren does not respond.*

I mean—I can't believe it…! I can't believe that you would give me something that means this much to you—I don't even know what to say.

WARREN. Good.

> *She puts it on her head and self-consciously "models" it for him.*

JESSICA. What do you think?

WARREN. …Looks great on you…

JESSICA. You think?

WARREN. Definitely.

> *She looks at him. He is clearly in distress and can't hide it.*

JESSICA. Well, you look totally miserable.

WARREN. I'm not.

JESSICA. *(Taking off the hat.)* Well I'm sorry, but I feel really weird taking your grandfather's hat.

WARREN. Then why'd you fucking ask me for it?

> *Jessica flushes a deep mortified red.*

JESSICA. I was *totally kidding*
when I asked you for something—   WARREN. No you weren't!

JESSICA. Yes I *was*! And then you *insisted* I pick something! Only why did you *give* it me if you don't want me to *have* it!?!

WARREN. Because I really want you to have it!

JESSICA. But why do you keep SAYING that when you obviously DON'T!?

65

WARREN. NO! God *damn*! What do I have to do, like *BEG* you to take it from me?!

A long moment.

JESSICA. OK. Sorry.

She puts the hat back on her head. Silence.

Well… I mean… Should I just go home?

WARREN. *(Looking at the floor.)* I don't know… Do whatever.

JESSICA. Well, then I guess I will.

She goes to the door.

Should I assume you no longer want to go out this week?

WARREN. I don't think we can. I'm all out of baseball hats.

Jessica takes off the hat.

JESSICA. Can I please say something?

WARREN. You try to give me that hat back one more time, I swear to God I'll fuckin' *burn* it!

Pause. Jessica puts the baseball cap down on the table.

JESSICA. Well… That would be up to you.

She turns and exits. Warren stands very still for a minute. Then he gets up and carefully puts the hat with his stuff. He sits at the table and very carefully dumps all the cocaine on the dinner plate and looks at it. He spoons some mannitol onto the plate and starts mixing the two powders together, concentrating intensely. The phone rings. He reaches for it and knocks the entire plate of cocaine onto the floor. He doesn't know what to do for a minute. He laughs. The phone keeps ringing. He answers it.

WARREN. *(Into the phone.)* Hello?

He stands up like he just got an electric shock. He listens for a moment.

Well, Dad, I guess the jig is up… N—… Well could I—… No I—… I was planning on *returning* it… Thank you… Well, you're actually gonna have to wait like an hour… Do whatever you want, but I won't be here… Why don't you punch me in the face and throw me out of the apartment?… That is definitely my intention… Uh huh… I don't know, Dad: What kind of world do *you* think I'm living in?...

Pause. He sits down. More quietly.

Yeah. I think about her all the time... I don't really know, Dad. I just see her in my imagination, I guess... Well, I feel pretty strongly about the fact that I have a lot better judgement than she did at my age, and it's also not too likely that I'm gonna move in with some thirty-five-year-old guy who beats me up all the time. So I don't really think it's an appropriate comparison. Although I will say that it's a totally obvious one. By which I mean I don't think it's all that clever... All right: I know your brunching companions await... Well, it is really hard to fully appreciate what your girlfriend has to go through, but it's really fucking fortunate that she has both the good looks and the intelligence to see her through all the rough spots... Sounds good... Do whatever you want... I hate you too.

> *His father hangs up. Warren hangs up too. He looks at the cocaine on the floor. He starts to scrape what he can off the floor and onto the plate. But it's an impossible job. He suddenly stomps on the cocaine, smearing it all over the floor with wild kicks. After a moment of this, he stops. Dennis comes in, very freaked out. He puts down the suitcase, now empty.*

DENNIS. What are you doing? What happened?

WARREN. I knocked the drugs on the floor.

DENNIS. You did *what*?!?

WARREN. I was trying to mix in the cut.

DENNIS. What?!? How bad is it?

WARREN. It's pretty bad.

DENNIS. Oh—GOD! OK—All right—I can't even deal with this right now—Listen to me, Warren. Something terrible has happened.

WARREN. What's the matter? Somebody's dead?

DENNIS. Yeah.

WARREN. Who, my mother?

DENNIS. *(Furious.)* No, not your *mother*, you idiot—

WARREN. OK—!

DENNIS. It's *Stuey*.

WARREN. Who?

DENNIS. Stuey! Stuey! It's fuckin' Stuey!

WARREN. Stuey who?

DENNIS. Stuart! The Fat Man. Stuart Grossbart. What's the matter with you?

WARREN. Oh shit. *That* Stuey.

DENNIS. Yeah "that Stuey"!
How many fuckin' Stueys do
you know?

WARREN. All right! I couldn't place the name for a second! What happened to him?

DENNIS. I don't know, man. I guess he did too many speedballs. He was with that Dutch chick all night and they went to sleep and when she woke up this morning she couldn't wake him up, so she turned him over and there was blood coming out of his nose and his *eyes*, and he was dead.

WARREN. Whoa.

DENNIS. I mean I just *saw* the guy last *night*. I am so freaked out. I can't even believe it.

WARREN. How did you find out about it?

DENNIS. 'Cause when I got to Donald Saulk's house he was on the phone with Yoffie. So I got on the phone and Yoffie told me he went over to Stuey's this morning and there were all these cops there, and that girl was sitting there freaked out of her mind crying and screaming and like smoking cigarettes and talking half in English and half in Dutch, and Yoffie told the cops he was Stuey's friend and they told him what happened.

WARREN. *Stuey*.

DENNIS. I guess it's a good thing we didn't do any speedballs. You know?

WARREN. But did we buy bad shit, or what?

DENNIS. I don't think so. I was doing it all night and I didn't wake up with fuckin' blood coming out of *my* nose. Did you?

WARREN. No. But I didn't do any of it yet.

DENNIS. And the *girl* was OK. So I guess he just overdid it. But I am so freaked out. I mean the guy is *dead*. Do you know what that *means*? It's like, he's not gonna be *around* any more, like at *all*. And it's just got me really fuckin' scared. I mean we are such assholes to be doing all this shit, man. I am totally stopping. I know he was a big fat slob who totally overdid everything and all he ever ate was like sirloin drenched in butter and sour cream, but the guy was like twenty three years old and now he's just *gone*. You know? Like he is no *more*.

WARREN. Yeah.

DENNIS. I don't know, man. I guess there's only a certain amount of time you can keep doing this shit before shit starts to happen to you. I mean I am really scared.

WARREN. So did you sell my stuff?

DENNIS. Yeah.

WARREN. Did you have to sell everything?

DENNIS. Oh yeah.

WARREN. How much did you get for it?

DENNIS. I only got nine hundred.

WARREN. What do you *mean*?!

DENNIS. I mean you had a totally inflated idea of what that shit was worth, so don't make me feel *bad* about it—

WARREN. I know *exactly* what it was worth and that guy just rooked you.

Dennis turns white with rage.

DENNIS. I am really gonna fuckin' hit you, man! I totally got you the best possible deal I could!

WARREN. Then you shouldn't have *sold* it!

DENNIS. You *told* me to sell it! At least I didn't knock the fuckin' *coke* on the floor, so don't make me feel *bad* about this, man, all right? I'm freaked out of my mind. So maybe I didn't do so well. I don't know. I'm sorry. It's better than nothing.

WARREN. I guess.

Silence.

DENNIS. What happened to that girl?

WARREN. She left.

DENNIS. You already had a fight with her?

WARREN. I'm not really sure what happened.

DENNIS. How could you mess that up so fast? What kind of talent for misery do you have, man?

WARREN. I don't know. I guess I'm pretty advanced.

DENNIS. Did my girlfriend call back?

WARREN. No.

DENNIS. I think I went too far with her before. But I can't even deal with it right now. I'm too freaked out.

Dennis lies down on his back.

I just can't believe this, man, it's like so completely bizarre. And it's not like I even liked the guy that much, you know? I just *knew* him. You know? But if we had been doing those speedballs last night we could both be *dead* now. Do you understand how *close* that is? I mean… It's *death*. *Death*. It's so incredibly heavy, it's like so much heavier than like ninety-five percent of the shit you deal with in the average day that constitutes your supposed life, and it's like so totally off to the *side* it's like completely ridiculous. I mean that was *it*. That was his *life*. Period. The Life of Stuart. A fat Jew from Long Island with a grotesque accent who sold drugs and ate steak and did nothing of note like whatsoever. I don't know, man. I'm like, high on fear. I feel totally high on fear. I'm like—I don't even know what to *do* with myself. I wanna like go to *cooking* school in *Florence*, or like go into *show* business. I could so totally be a completely great chef it's like ridiculous. Or like an actor or like a director. I should totally direct movies, man, I'd be a genius at it. Like if you take the average person with the average sensibility or sense of humor or the way they look at the world and what thoughts they have or what they think, and you compare it to the way *I* look at shit and the shit I come up with to *say*, or just the *slant* I put on shit, there's just like no comparison at all. I could totally make movies, man, I would be like one of the greatest movie makers of all time. Plus I am like so much better at sports than anyone I know except Wally and those big black basketball

70

players, man, but I totally played with those guys and completely earned their respect, and Wally was like, "Denny, man, you are the only white friend I have who I can take uptown and hang out with my friends and not be *embarrassed*." Because I just go up there and hang out with them and like get them so much more stoned than they've ever been in their *life* and like am completely not intimidated by them at *all*. You know?

WARREN. Yeah.

DENNIS. I'm high on fear, man. I am completely stoned out of my mind on fear. And like you guys think I'm like totally confident and on top of it, but it's not true at all. My fuckin' mother is so fuckin' harsh and wildly extreme that I just got trained to snap back twice as hard the minute anybody starts to fuck with me. That's how I fight with Valerie. Like the minute we get into an argument whatever she says to me I just *double* it and totally get in her face until she backs down or like has to like, leave the *room*. And it completely works too, because I don't have to take any of the shit I see all my male friends taking from their fuckin' girlfriends, or like the shit my father takes from my mother. I mean all he does is fuckin' lord it over everybody man, over all my brothers and sisters and like all his fuckin' assistants and his dealers and agents and like all these fuckin' celebrities who buy his art, because he totally knows that he's like a complete living genius and so he's like, "Why should I spend two minutes talking to anybody I don't *want* to?" Except now he's like torturing everyone constantly because he basically never doesn't have to pee, and my mother is freaking out because she's working fourteen hours a day because they cut the money out of all her programs and she's totally predicting major inner city catastrophe in years to come, and she completely has his balls in a vice. She's like, "Eddie, you're an asshole. Eddie, nobody gives a shit if you have to pee: You always have to pee, so shut up." She just *tramples* him, man. She's like, "No matter what you do it doesn't matter, because all you do is sell a bunch of paintings to like one percent of the population and I'm out there every day like, saving children's *lives* and trying to help real people who are being destroyed by Ronald *Reagan*— So whatever you do and however famous you are it's just a total tissue of conceit, because it's got nothing to do with anybody but rich people." She just makes total emasculated mincemeat out of him and the only thing he can do to fight back is go fuck some twenty year-old groupie, only now he can't do that anymore because he's so sick, so he's just totally in her power, and all he can do is torture her from like a totally weaker position, and she's like laughing in his face. My family is sick, man, they're *sick*. You think your fuckin' father is crazy? What if like everywhere he went total strangers like worshiped him as a *god*? Wait till his *health* starts to go. Can you imagine what that's like? Like seriously, what does that *feel* like, to be looking ahead like five years and not knowing whether you're still gonna *be* here? You can totally see why people are religious, man. I mean how much better would it be to think you're gonna be *somewhere*, you know? Instead of absolutely nowhere. Like *gone*, forever.

> *Pause.*

That is so fuckin' scary. I am so fuckin' scared right now.

> *Pause.*

I gotta call my girlfriend. You have totally fucked me up, by the way. How emblematic of your personality is it that you walk into a room for *ten minutes* and break the *exact* item calculated to wreak the maximum possible amount of havoc, no matter where you are? You're a total troublemaker, Warren. I should totally ban you from my house. I am so keyed up. I can't shut up. I wish Valerie was here. Maybe I should call that girl Natalie and see if she'll come over and give me a blowjob. She really likes me, man. She told my sister I had beautiful eyes.

> *Pause.*

I do have totally amazing eyes. They're a completely amazing, unique shape. Like most people with my kind of eyes aren't shaped like this at all. My eyes are like totally intense and direct. Like if I look people in the eye, like nine out of ten people can't even hold my *gaze*. Did you do any of that coke?

WARREN. Not yet.

DENNIS. I don't even want to *look* at it, man. I'm so freaked out. I totally feel like donating it to *charity* or something.

He laughs.

That is so not funny… I wonder if anybody told his family.

WARREN. I'm sure they did.

DENNIS. I wonder if they'll have a funeral.

WARREN. I'm sure they will.

DENNIS. That's gonna be one big casket. I wonder if anybody'll show up.

WARREN. Why wouldn't they?

DENNIS. Because nobody *liked* the guy! I called like six people, and I was so freaked out, and nobody cared at all. They were all like, "Wow. That's amazing. Is the coke all right?" Now, I don't know if that means they're all like totally callous and unfeeling or whether the guy was just a totally reprehensible human being.

WARREN. Well, he didn't really leave me with any lastingly warm impressions. I mean, I'm sorry he's dead, but I read the *newspaper* this morning, too, you know?

DENNIS. Well, all I know is if *I* had a fuckin' funeral, there wouldn't be room to *sit*. Someday I'm gonna make a movie about all of us, man. Like if you made that guy Donald Saulk a character in a movie, with all that shit in his apartment, how heavy would that be? And most people would like find some bad actor to like do some caricature sitcom imitation of this guy and like totally miss all the intense subtleties and qualities of his personality, and if it was me I would just go in there and use the real *guy*, and it would be so much heavier, and so much funnier. Don't you think?

WARREN. I don't know.

DENNIS. But don't you think I would be like an amazing director?

WARREN. I have no idea, man.

    Pause.

DENNIS. What do you mean you have no idea?

WARREN. I mean I have no idea.

    Pause.

DENNIS. Well I totally would be. I would totally—

WARREN. But you've never *done* it.

DENNIS. What do you mean?

WARREN. I mean you've never *done* it. You don't know anything *about* it. You just like movies. And have an interest in people's personalities.

DENNIS. No I don't "just like movies." I totally—

WARREN. *(On the 2nd "I.")* I like them too. But I don't necessarily think you'd be a good movie director, because I have no idea if you have the slightest talent for it whatsoever. I'm sorry.

DENNIS. You are really pissing me off.

WARREN. I don't really give a shit, man. Why did you sell my fuckin' toy collection for nine hundred dollars?

DENNIS. Is that what you're mad about? With poor Stuey moldering in the ground?

WARREN. I don't give a fuck about Stuey and neither do you. I didn't even *know* him.

DENNIS. So call the guy up and get it back and dig your own fuckin' grave, you little asshole! I am totally sick of you and your moronic fuckin' self-imposed *dilemma.* I've been dealing drugs for five years and I never *once* dropped any of it on the fucking *floor!* Because I am not an *imbecile!* I cannot believe that you *do* that, and then you have the nerve to give me shit because I undersold your little *toy* box!

> *Pause.*

WARREN. Why do you have to talk to me that way, man?

DENNIS. Why do I talk to you what way?

WARREN. Why do you have to call me an asshole like every five seconds? I don't like it.

DENNIS. What do you mean? We call each other shit all the time. Don't start with me, Warren, because all I've been doing for the last two days is like totally try to help you!

WARREN. I know you're doing *something*, man. But I can barely tell if you're even on my *side.*

DENNIS. What are you *talking* about? I'm on your side, I'm *totally* on your side.

WARREN. Then why are you always like, reminding me that I haven't done well with girls for a really long time, man?

DENNIS. Because—

WARREN. And like constantly insulting me and like *teasing* me and like telling me how incompetent I am and what a fuck-up I am, like this running motif like *every time* we hang out?

DENNIS. Because you *are* a fuck-up. So am I! So is everyone we *know*. What is the big deal?

WARREN. And how come every time I said I liked a girl you immediately say she's got a fat ass, or like has no tits or she's got a horse face or whatever. You know? Jessica Goldman is the first girl I ever had a chance with who was like clearly good-looking enough that you weren't able to make me feel like a second-rate asshole for wanting to go out with her.

DENNIS. You are really making me mad. That's what you're mad about? Because of that time I said that girl Susan had a horse face? That's just the way I talk, man. We *all* talk that way, it doesn't mean anything. You can't like suddenly turn around and act all fuckin' hurt and sensitive about that shit, that's the way we *are* with each other. Besides, that girl Susan *did* have a horse face, and everybody else could *see* it. I'm just the only one who *says* it. And when you're with a really good-looking girl I fuckin' say *that*. So don't give me this shit from the back *benches* of the fuckin' *peanut* gallery because it's total bullshit, and I am already so sick of you after hanging out with you for less than twenty-four hours in a row that I'm like two seconds away from beating the fucking shit out of you, you little fuckin' asshole!

Pause.

What do you *mean* I'm not on your *side*?!?

WARREN. I'm sure you love me, man, and you're totally like my personal hero, but I really don't get the feeling that you are.

A moment. Dennis gets up. His face twists into a strange shape and then he breaks out with a surprising choking sob. He starts crying. This goes on for a moment. Warren watches him coldly.

What are you crying about?

DENNIS. What do you *think* I'm crying about?!

WARREN. I assume you feel bad about something you think has happened to you.

DENNIS. *No...* It's because you said I was your hero.

WARREN. Oh.

> *Dennis goes to the kitchenette and blows his nose with a paper towel. Pause.*

DENNIS. So what are you saying? You want to like, stop being friends with me?

WARREN. I don't know, man. I'm not like, breaking *up* with you... I'm not your *girl*friend.

DENNIS. So what are you saying?

WARREN. I don't know.

> *Silence.*

DENNIS. Well... I can't really...

> *Silence.*

WARREN. Let's just drop it.

DENNIS. All right.

> *Silence.*

WARREN. Can I have that money?

> *Dennis gives Warren the nine hundred dollars.*

Well... I'm only eighteen hundred short.

DENNIS. Well—I'll start moving what's left of this shit today and see how much we can scrape up.

WARREN. It doesn't matter.

> *Silence.*

DENNIS. You wanna smoke pot?

WARREN. All right.

> *Dennis goes to his table and takes out a small plastic bag of pot.*

Where did you get that?

DENNIS. I got it from Stuey last night. Christian sold him some. I'd still like to find out where Christian got it. It fuckin' pisses me off that these ragamuffins are like running around copping drugs that I don't know about. I was gonna get some of that heroin from Stuey till it killed him. I just hope it's understood in the community that this coke is like, really good and that Stuey just overdid it.

WARREN. I'm sure it is.

Dennis starts rolling a joint.

It is sort of amazing that one of us actually died. You know?

Pause.

It's like my dad's always saying, "Do you know how *bad* you guys would have to fuck up before anything really serious ever happened to you?

Pause.

You and all your friends from the Upper West Side who went to that fuckin' school where they think it's gonna cripple you for *life* if they teach you how to *spell*?

Pause.

Do you know what happens to other kids who do the kind of shit you guys do? They *die*, man. And the only difference between you and them is *my money*... It's like a big fuckin' safety net, but you can't stretch it too far, man, because your sister fell right through it."

Pause.

But the fact is, he's just so freaked out of his mind that he did so well, and it all blew up in his face anyway. Like he did this great enterprising thing for himself and his family, and made a fortune in this incredibly tough racket, and got a house on the Park without any help from anyone, and he never felt bad for anyone who couldn't do the same thing. But when he was at the height of his powers, he totally lost control of his own daughter, and she ended up getting beaten to death by some guy from the world next door to us. And there was nothing he could do about it.

Pause.

So...for the last nine years, he's been trying to literally pound his life back into shape. But it's not really going too well, because he's totally by himself.

Pause.

You know?

DENNIS. I guess.

> *Pause.*

I can't believe you don't think I'm on your *side.*

> *Pause. Warren looks at him as if from a very great distance.*

WARREN. All right, all right. You're on my side.

DENNIS. *(Lighting up.)* So? What are you gonna do?

WARREN. I don't know, man. I guess I'll just go home.

> *Dennis smokes pot. Warren sits there. The lights fade out.*

End of Play

PROPERTY LIST

(Use this space to create props lists for your production)

SOUND EFFECTS

(Use this space to create sound effects lists for your production)

Note on Songs/Recordings, Images, or Other Production Design Elements

Be advised that Dramatists Play Service, Inc., neither holds the rights to nor grants permission to use any songs, recordings, images, or other design elements mentioned in the play. It is the responsibility of the producing theater/organization to obtain permission of the copyright owner(s) for any such use. Additional royalty fees may apply for the right to use copyrighted materials.

For any songs/recordings, images, or other design elements mentioned in the play, works in the public domain may be substituted. It is the producing theater/organization's responsibility to ensure the substituted work is indeed in the public domain. Dramatists Play Service, Inc., cannot advise as to whether or not a song/arrangement/recording, image, or other design element is in the public domain.

NOTES
(Use this space to make notes for your production)

NOTES

(Use this space to make notes for your production)

NOTES
(Use this space to make notes for your production)

NOTES
(Use this space to make notes for your production)

NOTES

(Use this space to make notes for your production)

NOTES
(Use this space to make notes for your production)

NOTES
(Use this space to make notes for your production)